UN

Book Three

Somewhere In The South Pacific

32nd Division (15,000); 126th Regiment (4,000);
3rd Battalion (1,000); Company I (230)
371-11-184

Michael Timothy Cavanaugh

SOMEWHERE IN THE SOUTH PACIFIC
2017 by Michael Timothy Cavanaugh

ISBN 13: 978-1973831211
      10: 197383121X

First Edition

The
<u>UNDAUNTED QUEST</u>
Series

Book 1 — *The Patience*

Follows the spiritually motivated journey of two German families from their beloved but conflicted homeland to the shores of an unformed country in the mid-eighteenth century.

Book 2 — *The Rock of Molum*

The Irish exodus through the experiences of four immigrant Irish families to America on the heels of the Irish Potato Famine.

Book 3 — *Somewhere in the South Pacific*

The story of a WWII GI who gave his life at the Huggin's Roadblock on the Sanananda Trail during the battle known as Buna, New Guinea.

Book 4 — *Strength Instilled*

A story of growing up on an Iowa farm, a life now known only in the history books.

Book 5 — *Weakness Embraced*

Underscores a fundamental lesson learned over a lifetime.

Acknowledgements

To my father, Clem; my grandfather, Bill; and my great-grandfather, John. They embraced their pasts and captured their moments to secure a better future for themselves and their posterity. These men had incredible work ethics forged in rural Iowa while farming with horses. They rose to every challenge including immigration, learning a new language, raising many children, the Depression, and World War II. My father served in WWII and lost his brother and two first cousins in that war, a high cost for one family but not unlike many in those days.

James Dietz is a contemporary artist who portrays historical artwork, particularly of subjects from the First and Second World Wars. His portrayal of the Battle of Buna is depicted on the cover of this book with his permission and my gratitude.

Jack Cavanaugh is a professional, award winning author. Jack has said, "The power of story is its ability to ennoble, to help us aspire to be better than we are," and he has accomplished that in the many books he has written. Thank you for your friendship, example, and your support in helping me prepare my books for publication, Jack!

Clem and Tim Cavanaugh, October 13, 1989

Dedication

Back Row (left to right): Paul and Erin Pavlik; Joyee; Fiona Cavanaugh; Luke and Caitlyn Bergman; Ben Bergman; Front Row (left to right): Chris Cavanaugh; Idelette Pavlik; Edythe Cavanaugh (101 years-old at the time of this photo); Jude and Jonah Pavlik; Will, Tori, and Ava Cavanaugh; Julie and Tim Cavanaugh; Margaret Bergman; Ryan Cavanaugh; and Morrow Pavlik. Not Pictured: Christian Clonch and November, 2017 Baby Pavlik.

To the posterity previous generations laid their lives down for. Might we never forget what they gave. Might we never tire of giving.

> Then you will call, and the Lord will answer; you will cry, and He will say, 'Here I am'. If you remove the yoke from your midst, the pointing of the finger and speaking wickedness, and if you give yourself to the hungry and satisfy the desire of the afflicted, then your light will rise in darkness and your gloom will become like midday. And the Lord will continually guide you, and satisfy your desire in scorched places, and give strength to your bones; and you will be like a watered garden, and like a spring of water whose waters do not fail. Those from among you will rebuild the ancient ruins; you will raise up the age-old

foundations; and you will be called the repairer of the breach, the restorer of the streets in which to dwell.

Isaiah 58:9-12

Table of Contents

Author's Note

The story of our family is one of converging families from numerous countries driven by religious conflict and undaunted in their quest for a better life for themselves and for their posterity. That quest abandoned kindred familiarity; invited dangers at land and sea; endured war and hardship; in tears buried their old and young; suffered and labored; believed and fought; faced prosperity and poverty; moved, settled, built, endured. Erect as dominos in formation behind us stand hardy stock from various backgrounds, who spoke different languages, were of different personalities, who habited diverse environments, and were of varying, Christian faiths. They pushed the next generation forward to a destination seen but through the eyes of God. Each individual of our family is a link in a chain of continuity impacted by those who have preceded them and guided by a powerful, loving God from whom all families derive their name.

Some of us have risen to the heights, others fallen to the depths. In our failures, there is nothing any one of us has done that, but for the grace of God, any one of us could have done. In triumphs, we all share, recognizing no height achieved is made possible apart from those whose shoulders we stand upon. We exist linked in familial community yet individually responsible to God for the life entrusted to us.

Part I of *The Patience* follows the Kunkles of Germany and their related families from Holland, England, Switzerland, Ireland, Scotland, and Norway in their journeys into the New World, many who helped establish the United States of America. *The Dakotas*, Part II, traces the journeys of the Shrivers and related families from their initial settlements in the New World into the adventures of the great American Westward Movement - a movement which began at the Alleghenies and five generations latter, with each successive generation of our family moving westward, ended in South Dakota.

It was in the western grasslands of that stark land that the Kunkles and the Shrivers converged into one woman destined for the fertile farmlands of Iowa and her marriage to a son of Irish immigrants as told in the story of *The Rock of Molum.*

As our family, many unknown to one another, expanded numerically into the thousands and geographically throughout America and to other parts of the world, the freedom which brought us to America and which we still so desperately cling to today, was tested in the fires of war. *Somewhere in the South Pacific* honors the life and times of one of our own who fell in that great conflagration known as World War II, a war fought against the evil of his day to preserve the freedom of ours.

Strength Instilled is the story of yet another generation of "dominos" pushed from behind by the generation preceding it. *Strength Instilled* captures a way of life known only in history books.

Two lives from that generation, both raised on Iowa farms, are portrayed in the book, *Weakness Embraced.* Their lives portray the many challenges to faith, hope, and love that face us all in a growingly complex world and our need for a strength beyond ourselves.

The day is drawing near when no force from behind and no momentum forward will link us with the past or with the future. The hour, as quickly as a vapor of breath, the weaver's shuttle, or the life span of a blade of grass before it withers, teaches us to number our days and reminds us we are but dust. The brevity of the moment of welcomed rest, stands in somber contrast to needful and prolonged, thoughtful reflection at the end of life - reflection meant to encourage, sustain, and push forward those who proceed and one day fill the ranks of our American family.

Moshe Dayan said it well in his autobiography underscoring that who we are is to a great measure who we were:

> The treads of a half-track rend a slope that has no name and is known to no one: Up comes an arrowhead three thousand years old. Dig again. Into the sunlight emerges a shard from the era of Joshua, the handle of a vessel from which a soldier of Israel once drank. Who was that man? He was myself.

Preface

371-11-184

Paul's high school graduation picture, 1934

By all accounts, Paul Cavanaugh was an exceptional individual albeit amidst human flaw. Had he not gone to New Guinea as an American GI, his life may have become as ordinary as any and known, perhaps, more for its shortcomings than its strengths. He did, however, go to and was killed in New Guinea. That extraordinary fact has punctuated his every ordinary experience and overshadowed every youthful short coming, ranking him among those we deem an American hero. Though Paul grew up in an idyllic, rural setting, it was the last months of his life, "somewhere in the South Pacific," that would define what his life came to be known for. This is his story.

Chapter 1

Conflict

New Guinea, an island second only to Greenland in area and the size of California is one of the wettest places on earth with 170 inches of annual rainfall (three times that of Seattle). November, December, and January are the wettest months in New Guinea with rain most every day at 3 p.m. and 11 p.m. Tropical storms called *Gubas*, boast of winds up to 70 m.p.h. and are known to dump one inch of rain within one minute. Kunai grass grows as high as eight feet with sharp, cutting fronds.

The country Uncle Paul never returned from had few roads, few trails, and vast uncharted areas. New Guinea reeked of stink lilies, contained swarming clouds of flies, chiggers, and sand flies small enough to penetrate mosquito nets. It was inundated with thick jungles and dank swamps ranging in depth from inches to over a man's head. Twisted, gnarled branches of bamboo, palms, and banyan trees were bathed in unbearable, sweltering heat. Average humidity levels hovered at eighty-five percent and average temperatures struck ninety-five degrees Fahrenheit. Within three miles of the shoreline, jagged mountains protruded from the earth and protected the interior from all but the most courageous of explorers, many of whom never returned from their exploits.

Within New Guinea's dense jungles, lurked man-eating crocodiles;[1] venomous snakes; pythons; poisonous spiders; malaria-infested mosquitoes (the soldiers were not issued insect repellant); giant fruit-eating bats called "flying foxes," not dangerous but detested by the natives, and Long-tailed Honey Buzzards - those constant reminders of death jokingly shrugged off by the men with a jibe,

"They'll be eating me tomorrow."

The country was infested with gigantic rats feeding on dead carcasses (not too infrequently human). Biting ants and teaming leeches left many a GI, slogging through the mud, periodically stopping to singe blood-engorged leaches from their groins and backsides with cigarettes and then asking their "ass-hole buddy" to inspect hard to get to spots. Paul was taught how to sit down on a log to avoid being bitten by something poisonous. Historian, Eric Bergerud called New Guinea, "some of the harshest terrain ever faced by land armies in the history of war."

More dangerous than the terrain or wild life was disease. Dysentery, ulcers from humidity and heat; jungle rot[2], Black River fever; jaundice, and anemia resulting from malaria breaking down red-blood cells; Yellow fever (also called Black Vomit), a hemorrhagic disease resulting in blood loss; trench foot; hookworm, a disease that afflicted Dr. Warmenhoven[3]; Dengue fever; leishmaniasis (characterized by open sores); beriberi; various forms of typhus[4], and fungal induced ringworm[5] were some of the tropical diseases the men were inflicted with. Sixty-seven percent of the 14,500 American troops involved in the three-fronted Buna campaign (Gona, Sanananda, and Buna) contracted malaria. The casualty rate jumped to eighty percent for those serving with Paul on the Sanananda front. In addition to all these ailments, there was malnutrition.

Subsequently, few journalists were willing to enter the uncharted jungles of New Guinea, resulting in fewer videos and photographs being taken of the Buna campaign compared to other South Pacific and European battles. One man from Company I, who fought in New Guinea and into other South Pacific campaigns such as Saidor, Aitape, Morotai, Halmahera, Leyte, and Luzon, told me that, for him, Buna was the most difficult campaign of all.

Apart from the environment, Paul faced another enemy, the Imperial Japanese Army. 3,300 Allied soldiers were killed and 5,500 wounded in New Guinea compared with 1,100 killed and 4,350 wounded in Guadalcanal. In the battle zone, a soldier's line of vision was often measured in feet. Battles were fought with grenades, bayonets, in hand-to-hand combat and, since the Japanese did not bury their dead, fought with the stench of unburied human flesh as a pervasive and constant reminder of what was at stake with every wrong move. Some Japanese fought with gas masks to screen the stench from Japanese bodies that were sometimes used as sandbags.

The supply line was the longest in U.S. Military history and the entire route by water which, at that time, was controlled by the undefeated Japanese navy who was sailing the Pacific Ocean at will. Charles Willoughby called the Pacific theater a "War of Distances." MacArthur was in charge of defending an oceanic area the size of the United States. What supplies did get through often didn't reach the soldiers, dropped from the skies but concealed by jungle foliage. Only nine percent of U.S. military resources were sent to the South Pacific. When Eisenhower invaded North Africa, he received 15 tons of supplies per man compared to MacArthur's five tons per man. For two months, the Allies attacked a nearly impenetrable enemy defense with hands tied behind their backs and with soldiers given minimal jungle training.

General Eichelberger[6], replacement leader of the Buna campaign, reflected:

> Buna was bought at a substantial price in death, wounds, disease, despair, and human suffering. No one who fought there, however hard he tries, will ever forget it. ... Fatalities closely approach, percentage wise, the heaviest losses in our own Civil War battles.

Eichelberger called Buna a "poor man's war" that was denied the backing of the American industrial machine: no bombardment of Japanese defenses by American destroyers, no tank carrying landing crafts, few supplies, little artillery. Kirkwood Adams, a gunner on a B-17, recalled:

> We used to fly up to Buna every day. That was a real mess. We went in low. It was terrible – you could tell that from the air. I'm glad I wasn't in it. It looked like the surface of the moon. Bomb craters all over – just

stumps of trees left. There was total devastation.
Things were so uncoordinated then. I think we
bombed our own troops as often as we bombed the
enemy. You couldn't see any terrain lines. They were
fighting so close.

Historian Stanley Falk said, "The Papuan campaign was one of
the costliest Allied victories of the Pacific war in terms of casualties per
troops committed." Even MacArthur later vowed, "There will be no
more Bunas," and he kept his word, having learned lessons the hard
way in the Buna campaign, one of the earliest battles and victories in a
land engagement against the Japanese in WWII helping to shatter the
myth of Japanese invincibility.

As reported in *The Ghost Mountain Boys*, a post-war gathering of
South Pacific vets speaks volumes and says it all regarding the rigors of
the Buna campaign. The vets were commiserating on the events they
lived through in the South Pacific. Sitting quietly to the side was
Stutterin' Smith, one of the Ghost Mountain Boys[7] and major of the
128th.

Without having said a word, Smith dawned his award laden jacket
and turned to leave. Intrigued, the vets caught Smith's attention and
asked him where he had served. A respectful, protracted silence
settled upon the room with Smith's simple reply ... "Buna."

Chapter 2

Iowa

One of my father's earliest memories was his preoccupation with a toy hammer in the front yard of our Iowa farm. Dad, just two-years-old, was playing at the feet of a man visiting Grandpa and Grandma. As Dad recalls, his eyes first saw the leather puttee around the man's feet and then followed the uniformed legs up the soldier's body until the doughboy's face was in view. He was a neighbor boy who had just returned from France during WWI. As Dad gawked at the soldier, Grandma held another infant son in her arms, fearful that the War might call Grandpa into battle. Little did she know then, the ones she should be concerned for was not her husband, but the son cradled in her arms, Uncle Paul, and his brother, Clem.

Tom and Mary (Wall) Cavanaugh

Paul's great-grandparents, Thomas and Mary (Wall) Cavanaugh, and his grandfather, then eight-year-old, John, emigrated from Molum Townsland, Kilmacow, County Kilkenny after being evicted from their farm in Ireland. They emigrated on the heels of the Potato Famine in 1851 or 1852. The family most likely walked to the Waterford docks then sailed either directly to the United States or, possibly, after a brief stop in England. They traveled down the Saint Lawrence Seaway, through the Great Lakes, and into the Waukegan, Illinois harbor. From there the Cavanaughs walked the final miles to the "Irish Plains," an Irish settlement just outside McHenry, Illinois.

According to Dad, Thomas Cavanaugh's wife, Mary, had a relative who married a Driscoll from Peoria, Illinois (Anna Carroll). Their daughter, Marian Driscoll, married Jim Jordan who, together, became the famous radio personalities, Fiber and Molly McGee. Dad recalled their visiting the farm when he was a kid. They signed with NBC in 1935.

Paul's grandparents, John and Mary (Gaffney) Cavanaugh and family (front row left to right): William (Paul's father), Mark (Mary's lap), John, Helen (became a nun), Harry; (back row, left to right): Elizabeth, Agnes, Roger and Anna McGowan (from Mary's first husband who passed), Mary; two twin boys (both mentally handicapped) and Mildred are not pictured.

After their father died of heat stroke scything wheat along the Fox River in Illinois, John and his brother William laid rail for the Chicago Northwestern from Chicago to Council Bluffs and on to Jefferson where John became the station agent. Together they bought farm land near Lohrville. Dad gave me the family anvil and vice brought with them from Illinois. Paul's grandma Cavanaugh died in 1907 of anemia. His grandfather Cavanaugh died three years later in a farming accident[8].

Bill Cavanaugh took his share of the inheritance and purchased the Cavanaugh farm after the farming accident killed his father in 1910.[9] Joe Miller remembered the convoy of farm implements traveling down the Crowley road in route to their new home which they most likely moved into on March 1, 1917. A few months later, on June 7, Bill and Greta Cavanaugh's fourth child was born, Paul Jerome. Paul would have four younger brothers and sisters in addition to his older three.

Patrick Butler Family (front row, left to right): Walter, Mrs. Butler, Mr. Butler, Isabelle, and William; (back row, left to right): John, Pierce (US Supreme Court Justice), Catherine, Cooley, and Emmett. Mrs. Butler was Patrick Gaffney's sister (Paul's great-grandfather's sister).

Paul's grandma Cavanaugh's parents, Patrick and Marie (Hatton) Gaffney, emigrated from Parrish Kilmurray near Roundwood, County Wicklow, Ireland, sailing through New Orleans up the Mississippi to Galena, Illinois before moving to Cedar, an Irish settlement in north central Iowa, not far from Lohrville. Patrick's sister and her husband continued through Galena into Minnesota[10]. Warren Harding appointed their son, Pierce Butler, an United States Supreme Court Justice.

Paul's mother's side all emigrated from Ireland as well. The Leonards and Hattons came through New York City and settled near Cedar; the Ryans and Caseys came from Ireland through Canada to Cedar. Caseys lived in Canada nearly 15 years before moving on rail through Chicago[11] just days after fellow Irishmen, Mr. and Mrs. Patrick and Catherine O'Leary's barn fire started the Great Chicago Fire of 1871 killing 300 people and burning down four-square miles of property.

Paul's maternal grandparents, William and Margaret Leonard.

Paul's older three siblings: John, Margaret, and Clem lived in Lohrville with grandparent Leonards during the school year in order to attend the Catholic school. Paul would often visit his older brothers and sisters at their grandparent's home in Lohrville. When the public school began busing kids, the family shifted schools from the Catholic to the public school, contrary to the Church's wishes. As one of the few (if not only) Catholic families in the public school at the time, the Cavanaughs felt a pressure to be as good if not better than all the other kids.

Paul's parents, William and Margaret (Greta Leonard) Cavanaugh

The Leonards raised Paul's cousin, Margaret Marie Fox. She remembered Paul and Clem as kids playing at their grandparent's home,

> Clem and Paul, ha, they were Irish imps. They would throw apples at Grandpa Leonard when he went to the outhouse just to keep him in there. Grandpa's only fault was his cussing and drinking. Grandma would holler at them to stop. They threw the apples because they knew he would swear. Paul and Clem were not alike at all but very compatible. Wherever one went the other was with him. They were different in looks. Paul had a wild nature. That was the difference between him and Clem. Paul would go to Carroll and go to dances. He'd meet girls. Clem was always a neat dresser. He'd find nice shoes and suites. As far as I know, Edythe was the first and only girlfriend he ever had.

Dad once told me how, as young boys, he and Paul tied cats together by their tails and threw them over a clothesline, amazed to think they could have done that. Perhaps Dad had a little hell-raising

in him too, at least when he was with Paul and in their younger years,
Paul and Dad worked hard. Dad wrote,

> By the time Paul and I were twelve or fourteen we did
> a lot of work around the farm. We could haul the
> grain away from the thresher, help load the manure
> spreader, pull the much-hated weeds and hoe some
> in the garden, though that was dangerous because we
> were prone to mix the weeds with the garden stuff.
> We also helped in the house some. ... Paul and I
> hauled more cobs from the hog yard for fuel for the
> cook stove than any two boys in Iowa.

Several of Paul's relatives entered holy orders. Paul's Aunt Helen
Cavanaugh, became Sister Stephanie and died just four months after
Paul. Paul's sister, Margaret (Sister Pierre), also entered holy orders in
the   Catholic
Church.   Bernice
Siemann, was the
third relative of six
women from St.
Joseph's Catholic
Church   in
Lohrville, Iowa to
enter holy orders.
Three   Gaffney
cousins   entered
the   priesthood.

St. Patrick's Catholic Church on Cedar, Churdan, Iowa

Father Louis Gaffney became the President of Seattle University, a
Jesuit college in Seattle.

Paul's first cousin, Bernice Chezlak, loved spending extended
stays at her Uncle Bill and Aunt Greta's home. She has fond
memories of the Cavanaughs and shared this account of the family:

> All the Cavanaughs were good at sports and would
> read all the time, but Clem read more than the
> others. They all were hard workers; none of them

were lazy. If there was a job to do it was done. No nonsense but full of fun. It was a happy house and everyone got along fine.

Though fun loving, the Cavanaugh kids were all highly ambitious and responsible by nature. Paul, however, was the lovable, hell-raiser of the bunch; brilliant, but not interested in going to college. His sister Marcella commented, "He wasn't interested in going to school. He was just one of those people who enjoyed every minute of every day. He wasn't eager to leave the farm. He liked where he was." Another relative wrote:

> Paul was very handsome, even more so in person than in his photographs. His hair complexion lent to an unusual beauty. I think his attractiveness was an internal quality as much as anything. He was unique, jolly, always happy, laughing, light hearted, clever, and fun to be with. If you were down and out, he'd pick you up. Paul was so comical. I really don't know anyone else in his family that had the same personality that he had. He was high-spirited.
>
> — Bernice Chezlak (first cousin)

> Paul was a wonderful, great guy. Very smart. His complexion was olive colored like Marcella where the rest of the kids were white. I think that color came from the Gaffney side of the family. He didn't look like Clem, more like Leonard but taller. Great sport. Played a lot. Worked hard. Paul went to mass on Sunday. We all regret what happened to him. We all loved him so much.
>
> — Margaret Marie Fox (first cousin)

As an old man, Raymond Melody reflected on the young Paul Cavanaugh he drove to Fort Des Moines with, on December 31, 1941:

God almighty – Paul never met a man he was scared of, good looking, friendly, wild, and a lot of guts. He held his chin high and wasn't scared of the devil. He didn't give a damn who knew it. He was an all-American boy, probably why he got killed so quickly. Paul had a high IQ and could have become an officer while at Camp Roberts, but he wanted to stay with the boys.

— Raymond Melody (Company C, Lake City)

Paul Cavanaugh

Paul grew up in a loving, supportive, and very large family. He grew up in an age when life was simpler: no electricity, no indoor plumbing, and farming with horses.

Jean Spenla, a younger cousin, shared how Paul rode into town on his bicycle one day. Jean commented to Paul, "I wish I could have a bike like that." Jean continued, "Paul looked at me for a while and then said, 'What the hell'? and gave me the bike! I guess he walked the 4½ miles home."

As Clem and Paul grew older, they worked and played together.

Dad continued in his memoirs:

Because Paul and I were both old enough and big enough to do a man's job we were frequently called upon to work by the day. We would help bale hay, sometimes cultivate corn, shock oats, and the hardest job of all, I think, was hauling manure. This was all pitchfork work. We worked for many different farmers. I think Paul mainly worked for Cliff Owens, that was steadier, while I worked on the shorter jobs.

Dad continued:

> In the fall of '32 Grandpa got seriously ill. He was in
> the hospital 90 days. I suggested to Grandpa that if he
> bought a tractor, they might not have to hire a man. I
> would be graduating and Paul would graduate the
> next May, and Paul and I could do the farming. For
> nine hundred dollars and three horses, Dad bought a
> tractor, disc, plow, spring tooth, and cultivator. Paul
> and I did the farming that year.

St. Joseph's school that the Cavanaugh children attended prior to the public school busing children. This building was used for catechism classes when I was a boy and is now the site of the "new" Catholic Church built in 1969.

Dad was a junior and Paul a sophomore when they assumed the farming responsibilities for Grandpa. Jim Clark (Clark Mollenhoff's[12] grandfather) showed Dad how to do the planting that first year. Cecil Siemann (first cousin) commented on Paul's physical ability, "Paul was very strong (not as strong as Clem). When the average man picked 80 bushels of corn in an hour, Paul picked 115."

Dad reflected on some of the fun activities his brothers and sisters would do:

Art, Aunt Annie, and Cecil came to our place after mass most Sundays. Cecil became a permanent member of our family. We played ball in the summer at Joe Spenla's, we went to Ross's hill (first farmhouse south of Vinnick's) to coast in the winter, sat in the kitchen reading western story magazines; worked in the big garden that Mom had a hard time getting us kids to weed and hoe. Paul and I, like all boys of the time, took catalogue paper and corn silk and rolled our own cigarettes behind the barn.

The Cavanaugh farm purchased in 1917. The barn burned down in 1963 and a new one built. Bill raised his family here and after the War, Clem and Edythe raised their family here (Mary, Pat, Sue, and Tim). Bill and Greta moved to the Clark farm, the next farm west.

Joe Miller said that Grandpa Cavanaugh was one of the first farmers in the area to plant soybeans. He baled the crop and stacked it east of the house. Miller said that Paul was smoking cigarettes behind the baled bean stack and accidentally started the stack on fire. The bean oil caused the stack to burn as hot as gasoline, according to Miller.

The bean stack was the first of many fires on the Cavanaugh farm. Grandpa and Grandma's home exploded and burned down years later (Memorial Day, 1972) destroying letters and photos Paul had sent to Bernice Chezlak while serving in New Guinea. Bernice had passed Paul's letters on to Grandpa and Grandma after his death. Two barns burned down within a week of one another in 1963, both during Fire Prevention Week (Vennick's and the home place). The Spenla farm house (Dad's place) and Strabala farm house (John's place) started on fire in separate incidents.

Mom relates a story of Grandma Cavanaugh combing her hair in the mirror of a vanity in the downstair's dining room on the farm. The boy's room was above the dining room (see the picture of the farm home on the previous page). When Grandma combed her hair in the vanity, the dining room window behind her was reflected in the mirror. One day, as she combed her hair, she saw in the mirror one of the boys fly past the window behind her.

The hog house was built in Paul's early years. In 1929, Henry Zinsmaster, admired by Dad and Paul for his construction ability, built the cement corncrib. The farmhouse was green and later painted white. John, Clem, and Paul shared the large room upstairs (Mary and Sue's) while Marcella and Marilyn shared the smaller room (Pat and Tim's). Ervin Amil was hired by Grandpa and moved into the Cavanaugh home in 1927, the year Leonard was born. John, Clem, and Paul shared their room with Ervin for seven years. Clem shared his bed with Ervin.

Lohrville, Iowa as it was in Paul's younger years. Note the absence of the "new" school wing which was built in 1959.

At one point, five Cavanaugh kids rode the bus together. In 1930, John was a senior; Margaret a junior; Clem a sophomore; Paul a freshman; Marcella was 11 years old; Clair, 7; Leonard, 3; and Marilyn would be born in 1933.

The Lohrville high football program started Paul's freshman year of high school in 1931. Those were the days you could fold-up your football helmet and put it in your back pocket, or so it seemed.

The *Lohrville Enterprise* gave these added insights into the life and times of Paul Cavanaugh during his high school years:

10/15/31, "Lohrville won the toss and acting captain McKinley elected to receive the punt. Paul Cavanaugh took the kick-off on the 30-yard line, went behind the four horsemen in the center of the field, and returned the ball to the 46-yard line. Sandburg, Waters, and Stephenson[13] took the ball from the 21-yard line around left end for the first touchdown. An unsuccessful kick failed to score the extra point."

11/5/31, "In the tackle positions were Albert Schroeder and Clem Cavanaugh; Schroeder, because of his size, blocked many a play on his side of the line. Clem, who is much smaller, made up for this by speed and determination, and as a result, he made many tackles behind the opponent's line. In the guard positions were Paul Cavanaugh and Stephen Gaffney (first cousins), both new, playing a good defensive game."

8/18/32, "About thirty people were entertained at a dance in the home of Mr. and Mrs. Wm. Cavanaugh Tuesday evening. Refreshments were served by the hostess."

10/13/32, "In the second quarter, Sandberg and C. Cavanaugh smashed through Lake View's line for nice gains, taking the ball to their 3-yard line when Paul Cavanaugh went through for their first touchdown."

10/20/32, "Pomeroy attempted pass was fumbled and recovered by P. Cavanaugh on their 35-yard line."

4/28/33, Paul's typing record indicated 48.4 words/minute with four mistakes.

Another newspaper article reads, "Paul played second base with a batting average of .286 just above Clem's .263 (the catcher). Paul Gaffney and the pitcher, Stephen Gaffney (Paul's first cousins), were batting .500 and .368 respectively." Esther Parker was in Dad's grade but had some classes with Paul. When asked her general recollection of being in a class with Paul, she said, after a long pause, "Let's just say, what an experience!"

Though there were many wonderful memories, in many ways, these were the darkest days of our farm, according to Dad. Grandpa found it very difficult to get the needed financing to pay the bills. They would succeed in keeping the family farm during the Depression but only by the narrowest of margins.

Weeks after Paul's high school graduation, on July 1, 1934, his grandfather, William Leonard passed away. Paul's Grandma Leonard would outlive Paul, passing away in 1952. Bernice Chezlak commented about the years following Paul's graduation from high school:

> Paul was a hard worker on the farm and dated a girl seriously from Carroll. He worked with Grandpa on the farm. There was no money in those days for travel so he spent some time right out of high school riding boxcars all over the United States. He sometimes slept in the community buildings at places he would go to. Sometimes a sheriff would even let them sleep in prisons. 5-6 guys traveled together.

In November of 2011, my son Ryan and I flew into Omaha in route to visit Mom. We arranged to visit with Bernice and Susan Chezlak. During our visit, Bernice shared that Paul's girlfriend of nearly two years was Delores (Dee) Wiederholt of Carroll. Ryan and I checked out phone books and saw a "Randy and Dee Wiederholt" living in Lake View/Auburn. We tried the number but it had been disconnected.

After Paul's travels throughout the United States on rail, he and his friends returned home, and Paul settled into farming with Grandpa. Clem and Edythe began dating in 1936, two years after Paul's graduation. Edythe recalls:

> The first night I had a meal with the family, I sat next to Paul. I asked for the butter, and he passed it to me. When I reached for it, he handed it to me "butter first" so that it smeared into my fingers. He had a very lovable personality but wouldn't give a dang about a thing. You might think of Paul as somewhat reckless by nature. At least at that point in his life, I would not have thought of him as a steady farmer. The bank wouldn't loan him money for a car without Dad signing for it. Of course, Clem was working in the post office then, and Paul was farming with Grandpa.

By 1937, Clem, Paul, Marcella (a senior), Clair, Leonard, and Marilyn were still living at home when Bill Strabela drove into the yard and offered Dad a post office job. Paul took up the slack Dad's absence created. It was nine years before Dad returned to farming. He worked at the Post Office for five years and then joined the Army Air Corp during World War II for nearly four years. Dad believed that had Paul survived the war, he might have operated the family farm instead of Dad.

On September 1, 1939 Germany invaded Poland commencing WWII. Paul's first cousin, Robert Cavanaugh[14], eagerly joined the war effort by enlisting in the Royal Canadian Air Force. He was killed in a

Halifax II Bomber; Robert Cavanaugh operated the top turret from which he shot out the port-inner engine (left side facing forward).

training flight in Great Britain and is buried in Saffron Waldon, Essex, England. The Royal Canadian Air Force informed Robert's mother, Catherine, of his death with this letter:

No. 405 R.C.A.F. Squadron
R. C. A. F. Overseas
November 23rd, 1942

File: 4058/408/56/P.I.

Mrs. C. Cavanaugh
1421 N. Quincy
Mason City, Iowa, USA

Dear Mrs. Cavanaugh:

By the time you receive this letter you will have been informed by the air ministry of the death of your son Sergeant R. J. Cavanaugh in a flying accident. We are writing you now to give you a few more of the details but regret that circumstances do not permit us to go too far in that direction.

The aircraft, of which your son was the Middle Upper Gunner, was detailed for a routine, daylight cross-country flight on the afternoon of November 17, 1942. We do not know just what happened but during this flight the aircraft got out of control and crashed in the south of England. We are convinced that your son did everything possible to prevent this accident.

Two members of the crew managed to bale out and with the exception of slight bruises, are safe. Unfortunately, your son and three other members of the crew did not have time to abandon the aircraft.

Your son and his crew were very popular on the squadron although they had only been here a short time and had not yet made an operational trip as a unit. You can understand, I am sure, that the loss of such a crew is very deeply felt here.

The funeral was held at RAF Station, Debben, Essex and burial at Saffron Waldon Cemetery, on the afternoon of Saturday, November 21, 1942.

Your son's effects have been sent to the Central Committee of Adjustment and will be forwarded to you after the necessary action has been taken.

We wish to extend to you our deepest sympathy in your loss and trust that if there is anything we can do for you at any time you will not hesitate to write us.

Yours very sincerely,

L. G. Fraser Wing Commander; Commanding, No. 405 RCA Squadron

Robert and the other three members of his crew buried side-by-side.

Robert Cavanaugh   George Gaffney

Paul's first cousin, George Gaffney, was killed in action off the coast of Japan onboard the *Pompano* submarine. The *Pompano* was very aggressive winning seven service stars and sinking many ships in its career. Its last patrol left Midway on August 20, 1943 bound for Hokkaido and Honshu. She was never heard from again. She did arrive in her assigned area, however, for two Japanese ships were sunk during September: *Akama Maru* on September 3 and the *Taiko Maru* on September 25, 1943. Since the enemy made no anti-submarine attacks during this period, it is presumed the *Pompano* was sunk by newly laid mines not known to U. S. Navy intelligence when she left Midway.

George was the oldest son of George Gaffney and Evelyn Wells. His father was one of ten children of James Joseph Gaffney and Julia Mary Mackey. George Sr.'s siblings included Bridget Dowling who died at 104; Veronica (Gaffney) Kavanaugh who married John Kavanaugh of Lohrville; and Blair Gaffney whose grandson, Francis Andrew Gaffney, became a medical astronaut and flew on missions into outer space. And so, Paul Cavanaugh and his siblings; Eileen Blaskovich; George Gaffney Jr.; and Clarence (the father of astronaut Francis Gaffney) were all first cousins.

In addition to Paul and his two first cousins that lost their lives, they had many other relatives who served and survived the War. Two female relatives served in World War II: Clare Agnes (McGowan) Gilbert and Maureen Shanahan Hallet, both nurses. Clare Agnes was given the choice between enlisting or being drafted. She chose enlisting as a second lieutenant nurse in the army and was based at Spokane, Washington. Maureen Shanahan Hallet was a nurse in the American Red Cross and served in North Africa, Italy, Germany, and France.

Cecil Siemann was an airplane mechanic based in the South Pacific Island of New Caledonia. John Dardis was in the fighting 29th infantry division and saw four years of action in France, Holland, and Germany. George Lynott Jr. was a combat engineer for three years in the Pacific. Thomas Francis Cavanaugh (Robert's brother) was stationed in India, Burma, and China with the Air Force. Walter

Butler was a second lieutenant of a tank division that crossed Europe into Germany. He was 30 miles south of the battle of the Bulge as it raged and was wounded by a shell blasting through the turret of his tank. Guy Blaskovich was based on Attu Island in the Aleutian chain keeping an eye on the Japanese. Jean Spenla served in the Air Force during the tail end of the war. Joseph Dowling did alternative service by working at a factory in Buffalo, New York building P-39's and helicopters. Paul Jerome Cavanaugh may have worked a short time with him until being drafted into the National Guard unit that would ultimately take him to his death in New Guinea. Blair Gaffney (from Lohrville whose son became a medical astronaut) served as a bombardier in the Army Air Corp. Jerome Cavanaugh was a stenographer in Germany and Japan. James Shanahan served in the Navy in the South Pacific. Terrance Donald Cavanaugh (Robert's brother) was highly decorated fighting in Asia and ultimately went to Japan. Paul Gaffney served in the Navy, and my father, Clement Cavanaugh (Paul's brother) was a bomber pilot and instructor.

I know Dad and Paul had their challenges working with Grandpa, though Grandpa was an honest, hard-working man with a great reputation in the area, he was definitely "old school" relative to Dad and Paul, and Paul was very youthful. Dad told me that Paul and Grandpa once got into a fight, which resulted in Paul taking a swing at Grandpa. Melody remembered Paul drinking too much at a party, a friend took Paul home and threw him over the fence where Paul remained straddled until the morning hours.

Chezlak recounted the day a visitor came to the farm. The husband was drunk and was making a scene around the sows. Grandpa was concerned enough to direct Chezlak, a little girl at the time, to go to the house. Paul resolved the dilemma. He put his arm around the guest's shoulders and talked with him as he walked him from the hog house to the corn crib where he subsequently locked him in the north corn bin until the guest sobered up. Paul was known to drink too much from time to time, but during my growing up years, I never saw Grandpa or Dad take a drink nor did we have alcohol in our home.

According to Dad, Paul and another guy from the area worked at an airplane factory fabricating airplanes in Buffalo, New York for a short time. I have a metal toolbox that Paul riveted from the same material the airplanes were made of. It was a job that could have kept him out of the military had he wanted it to. I also have a wooden toolbox Paul made in high school from pieces of scrap wood.

We get a great glimpse of Paul at home during Thanksgiving of 1941 in a statement from Bernice Chezlak:

> I spent thanksgiving of '41 with the Cavanaughs. I loved spending time with them. I spent three days there. Paul and I went hunting. I was 7-8 years younger. We hunted pheasants east of the corncrib. Grandma Cavanaugh[15] stressed being careful with the gun, so I walked 10 feet behind him. I carried a sack for the catch. Paul shot several pheasants and we put them in our bag. When the bag got too heavy, he carried it for me. It was freezing.

Paul fishing with his brother, John, in Minnesota during the summer of 1941.

Paul went hunting one day with less luck than his and Bernice's Thanksgiving hunt. Returning to the farmyard without a catch, Paul leveled his gun and killed a barnyard chicken then presented his trophy to the family.

Paul had tried to enlist in the military in the fall of 1941 but was told to wait until the New Year, according to the article in the *Lohrville Enterprise* that reported Paul's death. When Pearl Harbor struck, Paul was drafted or as they said back then, "selected" for service and inducted into the military on January 1, 1942. Chezlak said Paul didn't want to go but didn't complain about it either.

William, Greta, Leonard, and Marilyn at Mary Kunkle's home in Rinard. Mary Kunkle took this photo. Paul was at war at this time.

I wonder where Paul was when he heard the news that Pearl Harbor was bombed. I'm sure most young men knew their lives would never be the same. In a letter dated December 8, 1941 (Mom's birthday), Dad placed this letter in Mom's mailbox while working at the post office:

> My darling Wife,
>
> Today is your birthday. I have been thinking about it all morning. I think it would be nice if we could do something to celebrate it tonight, now that we have the car. If you think you won't go to Fort Dodge tonight, let's do something in honor of what may be our last birthday together for a long time. I know that we shouldn't think about it, but it seems to be so close today ... I don't know whether Dailey went with Paul last night or not. I tried to find out this morning but had no luck...
>
> With all my heart, Clem

Tuesday, December 30, 1941 was Paul's last night at home. We can piece that night together from several different accounts. Marilyn (8-years-old) and Leonard (13-years-old) were living at home and Marcella was home on Christmas break from the University of Iowa. Paul was 24-years-old and farming with Grandpa. After the chores, Paul drove to Lohrville for his scheduled hair cut from his barber: Mom. He returned to the farm, grabbed his best clothes, ironed his shirt, and picked up Marcella to go to McNabb's Dance Hall in Carroll. Aunt Marcella said they stopped at Scranton to say goodbye to Uncle Charlie, Aunt Susie, and their daughters, Bernice and Margaret Ann. Bernice remembered Paul being impatient to go because he was meeting "Dee"[16] at McNabb's. There was an up-and-coming band performing for the first time at McNabb's that night, someone by the name of "Lawrence Welk." Marcella continued, "The next morning (Wednesday, December 31) Paul and I met Lake City boys Raymond Melody and Merle Holm (pronounced hol-em) in Lohrville. They were inducted with Paul on January 1 in Fort Des Moines. Melody (Company C) would be seriously wounded but survive the war. Holm (Company K) would be killed nine days before Paul and in the same battle for the roadblock. The newfound comrades-in-arms would add George Frotscher of Farnhamville to their car and proceeded, in a snowstorm, to the railway station in Boone, Iowa. Chezlak recalls that Grandma Cavanaugh was upset with Marcella when she learned that Marcella dropped Paul and his fellow recruits off at the station and didn't wait to see them off, snowstorm or not.

The men proceeded on the train to Fort Des Moines where they spent their last night together as civilians. Melody said they were ordered to shovel sidewalks when they arrived at Fort Des Moines. Paul refused to shovel snow since he hadn't been inducted yet and hopped on his bunk bed and read magazines, according to Melody. After his induction the next day, Paul was assigned KP duty for the duration of his stay at Camp Des Moines.

Lawrence Edgington of Sac City joined the group the day they shipped out for boot camp, January 3, 1942. Edgington wrote

Marcella a lengthy letter detailing experiences he had with Paul in Boot Camp and in New Guinea and said he was ten yards from Paul when he was killed.

Fort Des Moines; Des Moines, Iowa

Chapter 3

Boot Camp

The men stayed at Fort Des Moines for three days and filled out paper work, were given shots by the "blood suckers" or nurses, took dental exams, and more. One man said, "We had our blood tested so often and had so many shots that it got to be routine." I have a copy of Paul's Fort Des Moines dental records used in New Guinea in an attempt to identify his remains. Paul weighed in at 180 pounds, 5' 7½" with an 8½ E shoe size.

Camp Roberts, California

Wednesday, January 3, was the start of a three-day train ride to Camp Roberts California, Paul's new home for the next thirteen weeks of basic training. While Paul went through basic, the 32nd Red Arrow Division of the Michigan National Guard was training in Boston, Massachusetts for a ground war in Europe. They had been told they would sail for Northern Ireland but were redirected to "somewhere in the South Pacific." They loaded into Pulman train cars and set their sites for the Cow Palace in Daly, California. One of the men said it was the greatest train ride he ever had.

Paul earned a reputation at Camp Roberts for being a great boxer. Melody said the Camp offered him a boxing position just to entertain the troops, but Paul wanted to stay with the boys instead.

Paul Cavanaugh at Camp Roberts. The license plate says "Virginia."

With basic completed, on Wednesday, April 15, 1942, a promised 30-day pass was revoked and the men loaded into trucks for a ride to the Cow Palace, a large enclosed arena at 2600 Geneva Avenue in Daly, California, a suburb of San Francisco. The Cow Palace opened in April, 1941 and immediately housed soldiers being shipped to the Pacific. Since then KISS, Elvis Presley, Metalica, the Who, the Allman Brothers, Fleetwood Mac, the Beatles, Santana, Neil Young, circuses, rodeos, plays, and sports events have been some of the many venues held in this 12,000 seat, enclosed auditorium which is still in use. It was here that Paul met the Michigan National Guard's 32nd Infantry Division based out of Grand Forks, Michigan. Many of the survivors of the 32nd still live in Grand Forks and meet regularly as lifelong friends who share a common bond few people could fully appreciate.

The soldiers received the newer styled helmets while at the Cow Palace, but Paul was issued the M1 Garand during basic training. Paul's M1 was one of 5½ million, 9½-pound rifles, with a walnut butt. General Patton called the M1, "The greatest battle implement ever devised." Paul's first response in being handed the gun was probably, "Damn, this thing's heavy!" In time, however, the adage, "The infantryman's best friend is his rifle," would be true for Paul who could take the gun apart and clean it blindfolded. The M1 worked when you needed it to: in the mud, sand, snow, or in rain. From the

San Francisco's Cow Palace

American Legion, September 1992 magazine article, "M1 Garand," you're taken to the firing range with these words:

> Breathe, aim, sight, squeeze, pow! Adjust the windage and elevation! Battle sight zero...You line up the sights on your Garand and squeeze 'em off. Eight quick jabs in the shoulder and pling! The empty clip signals reload time. Rock to one side to pull a fresh clip from your cartridge belt. Jam it in with your thumb. Ka-chunk! The bolt runs forward and locks up like a bank vault. Eight more ready to go.

M1 Garand with Bayonet

While at the Cow Palace, the men enjoyed San Francisco: China Town, Fisherman's Warf, trolley car rides and more. Then, on Sunday, April 19,[17] they left the Cow Palace for the piers of San Francisco.

The Camp Roberts boys joined the 32nd Red Arrow Division at the San Francisco piers to help bring their units up to wartime numbers. It was here, just before they boarded their transport ship, that Paul was assigned to his company. Units submitted their deficits and beginning alphabetically, the Camp

Eight-shell clip of a M1 Garand

Roberts boys were integrated into the Michigan National Guard's 32nd Red Arrow Division. This explains why *E*dgington - one of Paul's better friends, *B*eeman, and *C*avanaugh ended up in Company I; *H*olm from Lake City was assigned Company K; and *M*elody ended up in Company C. In a personal interview on October 9, 2011, ninety-nine-year-old Smested[18] said that his company's vacancies were filled with

men whose last names all began with the letter "S."

As the men boarded the ship, their last name was read off and, in response, they shouted out their first name and middle initial, "PAUL J."!! The soldiers always went by their last names even with one another. They were also given a one-penny post card to send home as they came onboard. The message was pre-printed for them, "Have arrived safely." I can picture Grandpa, Grandma, Leonard, and

Marilyn getting that card in the mail thinking Paul "arrived safely," when, in fact, he was just leaving San Francisco. The men loaded into several vessels. Paul's was the *Lurline* (a former Matson Luxury liner).

TYPICAL BARRACKS, CAMP ROBERTS CALIFORNIA

The *Lurline* in port at San Francisco's Pier 42 where Paul Cavanaugh boarded for Australia.

Chapter 4

At Sea

At 5:30 p.m. on Wednesday, April 22, 1942, the transport ships disembarked for "somewhere in the South Pacific." The *Lurline* shoved off from Pier 42. Their escort, the *USS Indianapolis* (pictured below), renown as the second-to-last ship sunk in WWII, departed from Pier 43.[19] The swimming pool was drained and converted into space for bunks and all the passageways were lined with them. Companies bunked together on board but officers got the best rooms.

The ship was filled beyond capacity and the men slept in "standees" (pipe frame bunks). They vied for space on deck when it became hot, especially as they approached the equator. The weather was great for the entire journey. Melody remembers flying fish accompanying their ship.

Ships could only go as fast as the slowest freighter, which was about 14 knots. In addition to the slow pace, they zigzagged making their trip a 25-day trip to South Australia. The boats would change from a zig to a zag every eight minutes operating under the principle that it takes eight minutes for a submarine to align its sights on a ship. Since a sub could never catch a ship, the ship was very safe zigging and zagging across the Pacific Ocean.

They stopped in Honolulu. Perhaps they had a chance to see the resent tragedy at Pearl Harbor, a visual motivation for the challenges that lay ahead. The above picture shows the *Lureline* arriving in port at Honolulu, Hawai'i. Paul would have experienced the disembarkation at Honolulu and enjoyed a few days there.

Everyone was in a jovial mood onboard, and the division orchestra played hit favorites such as "Tangerine" and the "Beer Barrel Polka." Popular singer, Frank Fisher, was also onboard to entertain the troops. General Harding himself attended the evening sing-a-longs. The 32nd found a dog onboard they named Vicksburg who became the mascot of the 32nd and eventually would die and be buried at Camp Cable, Australia. A monument marks his grave to this day.

Up until the Pacific voyage, the men only knew they were going to "somewhere in the South Pacific." In time, they were given an added clue, "somewhere that starts with the letter 'A'." On April 26, the troops were finally told they were going to Australia. The men needed to know in order to satisfy their curiosity, to stop rumors, and to begin lectures on adapting to the culture they would soon be living in. The lectures were mandatory orient-ation courses focusing on the

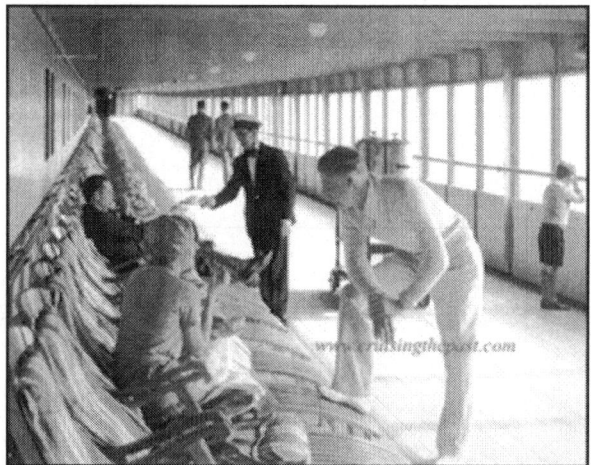

people and culture of Australia. The men walked the ship deck, did calisthenics, and played craps to fill their time.

They generally stuck together by companies, but one day Melody (Company C) and Paul (Company I) were hanging out together on deck. Paul looked over to Melody and asked if he were hungry. Melody said he was, and the next thing he knew, he was following Paul into the bowels of the *Lurline.* Melody told me they passed one "Do Not Enter" sign after another. Before long, they found their way to the kitchen, the refrigerator, and a great sandwich, just as the cook entered and confronted them for being there. According to Melody, Paul had the cook against the wall at knifepoint before they left, sandwiches in hand.

Missing May 7th altogether, the men crossed the International Date Line on May 6. As they approached the equator, the soldiers aboard the *Lurline* experienced the famed, Order of Neptune, a ceremony commemorating a person crossing the equator onboard ship for the first time. Such a person was called a "Pollywog" but after the crossing and an initiation, the Pollywog was promoted to a "Shellback."[20]

The Coral Sea Battle[21] forced the convoy to reroute itself from a Brisbane disembarkation to an Adelaide disembarkation. Flashes of the sea battle could be seen in the distance. The waters between Australia and Tasmania were the stormiest waters the soldiers had encountered. Finally, after three weeks onboard, with Adelaide in view, Paul and his comrades were nearing the end of their voyage. The impulsive, "act-now-and-think-about-the-consequences-later" sort of a guy, was approaching manhood.

Chapter 5

Australia

A delaide was, and is today, a big town with a lot of churches. It's ranked as one of the most livable cities in the world[22]. Some liken its weather to San Francisco's. The men speak of how beautiful their camp was, situated in wine country and surrounded by orange groves. Paul got to know a family from Prospect, a suburb of Adelaide. Today, the average home in Prospect sells for $750K. Dad remembers Paul writing of his interest in living in Australia one day.

As the men disembarked late in the afternoon of May 14, they were surprised by the hero's welcome they received from the throngs of people throwing flowers, blowing kisses, and crying. Young women lined the steps at the port. They were truly grateful the Yanks had come to help protect them from a potential Japanese invasion[23]. Paul celebrated his 25th birthday three weeks after landing in Adelaide.

By six p.m., the 127th and 128th headed east to Camp Woodside. Paul's 126th Regiment was trucked to Camp Sandy Creek, 30 miles north of Adelaide. The men stayed in eight-man tents at Camp Sandy Creek, clung to blankets at night for warmth, and made themselves as comfortable as possible on mattresses made of burlap bags stuffed with straw. On the brighter side of life, they could buy a bottle of wine for a shilling. The fact that Adelaide was under blackout orders was a constant reminder there was still a war going on.

The Australians had good reason to see the GI's as protectors. Between February 1942 and November 1943, the Australian mainland, domestic airspace, offshore islands, and coastal shipping were attacked over sixty times by the Japanese Navy and Army Air Force. Bombers, subs, and fighter planes strafed the camps. The first and deadliest attack on Darwin occurred on February 19, 1942 with 242 Australian deaths and Darwin being abandoned as a naval base. It was their version of America's Pearl Harbor. On June 8, 1942[24] a Japanese submarine shelled Newcastle, an industrial center on the east coast of Australia. The bombs struck the dockyards, steel works, Parnell Place, and other locations.

General Eichelberger commented that the Zero was superior in maneuverability to our planes, that the Japanese pilots were well-trained and highly skilled, radar in northern Australia was worthless, and we were outnumbered five to one. At this point in the War, the Japanese believed the War was practically over.

After three weeks on a luxury liner, the liberators became soft. Camp training included many hours at the rifle and machine gun ranges, throwing hand grenades, and engaging in mock wars. Lawrence Edgington and Paul were assigned a rotation of garbage pick-up together and probably wondered, "What does this have to do with winning the War?"

The soldiers trained with Australian fragmentation grenades, the grenades used on the roadblock (Paul's final battle). Many thought the Australian grenade more powerful than the American counterpart, more dependable, and quicker to explode - giving the enemy less time to pick-up the grenade and hurl it back. Rifle grenades could shoot a grenade into a slit-opening of a bunker with devastating effects. This weapon did not arrive to the Buna front until mid-December, after Paul's death.

During the weeks that the 32nd stayed near Adelaide, romances bloomed. Many Adelaidian women married GI's; some joined their husbands in returning to the U.S. after the War, with babies in tow; some returned on the *Lurline.*

During Paul's stay in Adelaide, Australians treated Americans like gold. When the GI's went to town for weekend passes, there were lists of families who offered to house them while they were in the city, since there weren't enough hotel rooms in town for all the men. when the train arrived in Adelaide from Sandy Creek, throngs of people simply grabbed a GI and took them to their home for a meal or even to stay the weekend. Perhaps that's exactly what happened to Paul on one of his weekend passes into Adelaide. A letter sent from an Aussie home to assure Grandpa and Grandma of Paul's well-being was published in the Lohrville Enterprise.[25]

Australian brides returning on the *Lurline* to the U.S. after the War. Many of these women met the *Lurline* with a hero's welcome when the 32nd came to Adelaide.

One Sunday night, a Michigan GI missed the train back to camp. He decided to stay another day since he knew he was already in trouble. He was demoted from corporal to private with a loss of $21/month in pay. Paul was already a private the day he and Melody missed the bus. They slept on the sidewalk at the train station. A restless Melody woke in the middle of the night and remembered seeing Paul sleeping like a baby on the concrete.

The Adelaidian train was so packed, men hung out windows. The train engine had no trouble bringing the men down to Adelaide from Sandy Creek, but the train could not get back to the Camp without some of the men jumping off the train to help it along.

Gawler (pronounced Gaw-la) was a small town in walking distance from Sandy Creek. If you missed the train you had gone to Adelaide. If you missed the bus (or walked) you had gone to Gawler. There's a bar there today with a sign overhead that says, "The 32nd was here."

Many Aussies were fighting in North Africa when the 32nd first arrived in Adelaide but some began to return before the 32nd left. The Aussies weren't happy with the American soldiers being there and many altercations between Aussie soldiers and American soldiers occurred in Adelaide, even some deaths.

After nearly one month in Adelaide and with the Japanese army descending the Kokoda trail to within 30-miles of Port Morseby, the 32nd's strategy was changed from a defensive war, protecting Australia from invasion, to an offensive engagement against the growing Japanese forces in New Guinea. The 32nd was ordered to load into trains for Brisbane to begin jungle warfare training in preparation for the New Guinea invasion. They would have to shift trains and transfer cargo twice in route since each state in Australia had different rail gauges. The first shift was at Melbourne; the second, Armidale. The train bypassed Sydney and took three days and three nights to reach their destination, a wooded area outside of Brisbane.

In July of 1942, the soldiers literally cleared a wooded area of gum trees and vegetation to make Camp Tambourine or Camp Cable, as it later came to be known. The men dug their own latrines, wells, built kitchens, and set up their tents. Camp Cable is located at Waterford Roads, Logan Village, 4207 Queensland. There is a monument there today which simply says, "U.S.A. Camp Cable; They Passed this Way." Whereas Paul was shipped from Adelaide via train to Brisbane, some men and equipment of the 129th and 120th Field Artillery units boarded 5 Liberty ships and sailed from Adelaide to Brisbane.

In route, one of the Liberty ships was torpedoed. Gerald Cable was its only casualty and first casualty of the 32nd Division in World War II. On August 30, Camp Tambourine was renamed Camp Cable in his honor. The diagram on page 52 shows the layout of Camp Cable. Paul's assignment was the section marked "126 INF," about four miles down the road from Division HQ, perhaps six miles from the nearest village of Logan, and on the same road you would take to Brisbane.

Gerald Cable, 1st Casualty of 32nd Division in WWII.

At Camp Cable, the Americans were instructed by the Australians what to expect fighting the Japanese in New Guinea. Paul was taught that the Japanese snipers tied themselves in trees and that in combat the battle wasn't just in front of you and at eye level. The enemy could be above you, beside you, ahead of you, or behind you.

The men were instructed in jungle warfare at Camp Cable. They were dropped in the middle of the wilderness with a compass to find their way home. If executed correctly, they would meet someone at a designated point. If not, they would wander through the wilderness all night long. Early in the morning, the men woke up to what sounded like a man but was a "Laughing Jack-Ass." There were eight-to-ten foot lizards in the area as well.

The 32nd got passes to beach towns like Tweed Heads and Coolangodda (coastal towns 30 miles south of Brisbane) just for fun. They rented horses and met girls. One GI bought a horse for a shilling (sixteen cents, U.S.) Melody and Uncle Paul rented horses and rode the beaches together, according to Melody.

At this point in their military training, many of the Americans were overly confident of victory. One soldier from Company I told me, "We thought we were Americans and that it wasn't going to be a big problem dealing with the Japanese ... We found out in a hurry that it would be a lot tougher than we realized."

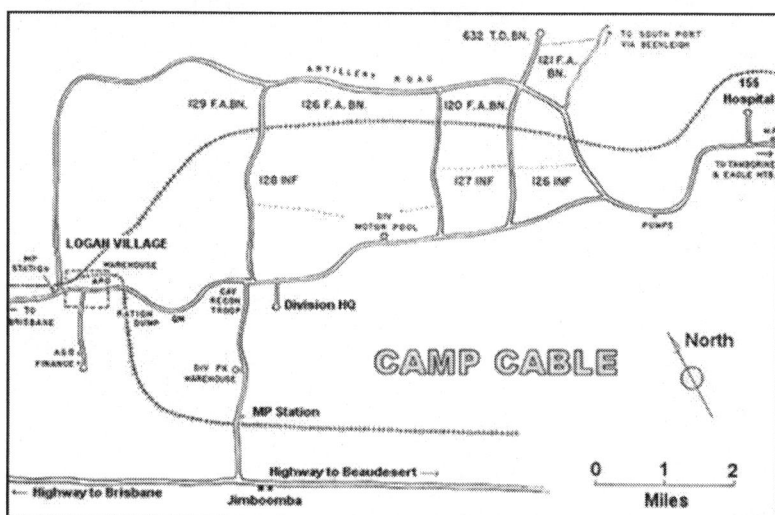

Edgington recalled sleeping with Paul in a tent when they received orders to move out about midnight. The men spent the next six weeks doing beach training on New Castle Island. They practiced land approaches in small rubber boats and scrambling up and down rope ladders on the sides of ships.

The War Department had a manual called the Watermanship Manual which instructed GI's on how to descend the life nets or cargo nets along the side of ships. These ropes served as ladders for disembarking into landing crafts or abandoning ships. Four to six men started over the ship's side simultaneously, left foot first. When the first line of soldiers had descended halfway, another line started over the side. Paul was instructed to grasp a single vertical strand with his feet on the horizontal strands on each side of the vertical strand he was holding. Alternately, Paul could grab each of the two outside strands in a group of three vertical strands with his feet on either side of the center strand. It was emphasized to Paul not to grab the horizontal strands to avoid a man above him from stepping on his hands. Each foot was to skip only one square at a time, longer steps slowed the descent.

Chapter 6

The Enemy

Thousands of years ago, the Chinese coined a word for the islands to the east of their country. They named them *Jih-Pen* meaning, "the source of the sun." The English word, Japan, derives from this Chinese word. Nihon (Nee-hone) or, when it comes to official business, Nippon (Nee Pone) is the Japanese word for their own country which also means "the source of the sun." The literal translation for the English word "Japan" is not, as some think, the "land of the rising sun," but literally the place where the sun originated.

The national flag of Japan depicts the sun which was also the symbol of their god-emperor who was a direct descendant of their sun god. The emperor was the religious and political leader of the nation and was not to be imitated. For example, during World War II, Hirohito's was the only maroon car in Japan. His personal tailor could not touch the Emperor. The Emperor was responsible for the growth of rice, justice, light, truth, prosperity, peace.

The Japanese soldiers Uncle Paul fought were taught the sun goddess, Amaterasu had a son, Ame no Oshihomimi no Mikoto. Through him, Amaterasu had a grandson named Ninigi. Amaterasu sent her grandson, Ninigi, down to rule the earth from Japan. Ninigi built a palace and married Konohana-Sakuya-hime and together they had three sons. One was called Yamasachi-hiko who married Toyotama-hime, the daughter of Ryujin, the Japanese sea god. They had a single son called Hikonagisa Takeugaya Fukiaezu no Mikoto. This young boy was abandoned by his parents at birth and raised by his mother's younger sister, Tamayori-hime. Tamayori-himi and Hikonagisa Takeugaya Fukiaezu no Mikoto married and had four

sons, the youngest became Emperor Jimmu, the first god emperor of
Japan who also received orders from Amaterasu to rule the earth.
From Jimmu on, Japan never wavered from their goal of world
domination, a goal or command called *Hakko Ichiu*. The Japanese
believed they were a superior race descended from the gods destined
to rule the world.

Hirohito, the emperor during World War II, was believed to be
the 128th descendant from Jimmu. All Japanese believed their blood
was comingled with the gods and therefore they had deity in their
veins. These beliefs set the stage for a people who believed, as did
Hitler's Germany, in the superiority of their race and in the dream for
world domination, not just the Pacific rim, the entire world.

Historically, the Japanese islands were divided into baronies or
districts led by barons. Soldiers that fought under their barons were
called samurai soldiers. The samurai carried two swords, a short one
to commit hari-kari if need be and another for battle. The lead baron
was called the shogun. Often in Japanese history, the actual political
power in Japan was held by the powerful barons and the shogun, not
the emperor. In either case, the goal was the same, world domination.

In 1592, the powerful shogun of the day thought Japan strong
enough to make a bid for Japanese world rule. China was to be the
first victim. The soldiers invaded Korea first. China came to the
Korean aid and the Japanese quest for world domination was forced
to wait for a more opportune time after the shogun was killed.

The Japanese saw another opportunity to fulfill their *Hakko Ichiu*
in 1894. They attacked and conquered Formosa. On February 8,
1904, they attacked Russia and defeated them, their first victory over a
world power. Korea was annexed by Japan in 1910.

The Japanese wagered the allies would win WWI and declared
war on Germany in 1914. The fruit of their wager was the acquisition
of Germany's previously controlled islands of Marshall, Carolina, and
Mariana. The Japanese seemed invincible and unable to make
mistakes. They won every war in the field and in politics.

Prime Minister Tanaka Gilchi may have formed a modern blue
print for *Hakku Ichiu* in 1927, the Tanaka Memorial. Although many

scholars believe this document a forgery originating from anti-Japanese
sources, others say it accurately reflected what Tanaka and many
Japanese leaders believed. Tanaka proposed Manchuria must be
taken first for their iron, coal, and other resources, then China for
people resources. He outlined that they would then go into Siberia for
wheat, coal, metal, and wood. From there they would bring Malaysia
under their control for tin. After these areas were brought under their
control, they would destroy the American fleet and advance to
California then on to the rest of the world. Tanaka supposedly
presented his plan to the Emperor, though when Americans searched
for evidence of war crimes after the War, no document was found.

Japan outlawed books, magazines, movies, and dancing, from the
West during the 1930's and only advanced Japanese culture. As
WWII approached, the Japanese promoted books like Admiral
Shinasaku Hirata's who wrote on March 13, 1930, "The attack on the
Hawaiian Islands must be the first battle in the war of the Pacific
Ocean." Japan began building up its military expanding the numbers
of planes, tanks, ships, weapons, and the army. Meanwhile, on the
other side of the Pacific, on a farm in Iowa, the fun-loving Paul
Cavanaugh was advancing from grade school, junior high, and into
high school.

One Japanese official wrote on September 18, 1931, "We can
land in Puget Sound, the Columbia River, the vicinity of San
Francisco, and the vicinity of Los Angeles but this is possible only after
we have destroyed the American, Pacific fleet." Another Japanese
authority wrote in 1933, "To save humanity in conformity with the
Great Spirit in which Emperor Jimmu founded the Empire, Japanese
should take over the management of Asia, then extend to the rest of
the world."

In his book, *Flyboys*, James Bradley writes of the Japanese
military milieu leading up to and during World War II:

> Hirohito entered the world at the dawn of the new
> era of Japan's military obsession. He was seventy days
> old when he was taken from his parents to be raised
> at the home of an elderly retired admiral to inculcate

the proper military values in the emperor-to-be. The Russo-Japanese War was the signature event of Hirohito's childhood. From his youngest years, he saw his grandfather, stately in his military uniform, basking in Japan's new status as a first-rate power. Hirohito was surrounded by military men and socialized to believe that military might was key to Japan's maintaining its place in the world.

Japanese emperors-to-be previously grew up in Kyoto studying ancient Chinese and Japanese text, poetry, and the like but remained isolated and powerless. Hirohito, however, grandson of the heroic infantry general of the great Russo-Japanese War, was trained in military strategy and promoted to a second lieutenant in the Japanese Army at the age of 11. Hirohito was taught that the epicenter of modern Japanese history revolved around his grandfather's heroics in the Russo-Japanese War. The Japanese were taught that their emperor was a god and, therefore, had to be obeyed. It wasn't, however, just the emperor who had to be obeyed; every officer, as the emperor's chosen elite, was also owed unquestioning obedience.

For example, school children would enter their classroom saying, "Sixth-grade pupil, third class Sato Hideo has business for teacher Yamada. May I enter?" Another student cried over dissecting a frog until they were reprimanded and reminded that they would need to kill 100-200 Chinks one day. Students walking past their teachers, stood and saluted them. In the military, Japanese trainees stood in the shower holding soap for their officers, scrubbed their backs, and fought for the right to untie their puttees at the end of the day.

Leading up to WWII, Japan sent agents disguised as tourists, laborers, fishermen, barbers, etc. to every country marked for conquest. On the day the Japanese invaded Pearl Harbor, Manchuria fell, Manila fell, Hong Kong fell, Singapore and Corregidor fell, and China was attacked. Colonel Hideo Ohira wrote during August of 1942, "Japan is firmly determined to fight a hundred years' war to crush the United States."

The Japanese celebrated the 2600 anniversary of the ascension of Jimmu to the throne in 1940. It was in 660 BC then, that he, the first god-emperor, began to rule in Japan and began his goal of world domination. Japan celebrates his accession to the throne every year on February 11.

A doctor T. Komaki wrote from Kyoto University on February 22, 1942, "From the view point of *Hakko Ichiu*, the Emperor of Japan is the Emperor of all the races of the world. There are not seven seas, all the oceans are to be recognized as the great Japanese Sea." In 1942, Washington and London seemed to struggle over Japanese intentions. Others, like General MacArthur, knew they were coming after us.

The national religion of the Japanese was called Shintoism which, during World War II, was the heart and soul of the Japanese people. Shintoism taught there was one emperor of Japan who descended from the sun god. Shinto, or "the way of the gods," defines how the Japanese drink tea, worship, arrange flowers. They also were taught there were 9 million gods (volcano god, lightning god, rice god, pearl diver's god, etc.). They believed there were 75 million living people and billions of living ghosts from deceased Japanese ancestors. These ghosts lived near the living and by clapping their hands, the Japanese could beckon their ancestors to their aid. Their ancestral ghosts would then help them maintain the way of the Emperor and helped the living to continue the path toward world domination.

With 400 people/square mile (compared to thirty-one people/square mile in the U.S.), the Japanese felt hemmed in and had an added incentive to fulfill their *Hakko Ichiu* or their "Eight corners of the world under one roof" command. They saw world domination as their world-wide, "Manifest Destiny" much as, in their minds, the U.S. had their Manifest Destiny of expanding from coast to coast. The militaristic mindset and their mission made the Japanese a formidable force as they executed their plan of world domination beginning with the Pacific rim.

First born sons, persons of property, bureaucrats, intellectuals, and others received deferments while poor farm kids were the ones drafted and the ones Paul fought. They were called *issen gorin* "one yen, five rin," referring to the cost of mailing a draft notice (less than a penny). Brutality and cruelty were the rule, not the exception, in the Japanese boot camp.

> Recruits were pummeled, slapped, kicked, and beaten daily. One recruit reports, "We were made to form a single line and stand at attention and then ordered to clench our teeth. Then they hit us with their fists." Part of their training included bayoneting a human. A circle was drawn around a prisoner's heart, they were tied up and the soldier was ordered *not* to stab inside the circle (in order to get multiple uses out of each prisoner). *Flyboys*, 39

The average Japanese soldier was 5' 3", 117 pounds. He was paid 10 yen a month or about $2.36. They have been likened to photographs that were all made from the same negative. Their fully packed load was 60 pounds, almost half of their weight. By American military standards, their uniforms were ill fitting, some comically so. Their drills lacked precision, but they knew their job. Their endurance was phenomenal. They were fed fish on occasion, but generally lived totally on rice.

Though paid little, the soldier was the highest position in the Japanese society. Perhaps their greatest strength was their faith in *Hako Ichiu*. Their faith justified brutality, rape, and torture against all non-Japanese races. They had a mystical belief that assaulting an adversary would in and of itself vanquish them, though their enemy possessed superior numbers and weapons. To the Japanese soldier, there was no choice between death and surrender. They would always choose death over surrender, for surrender would result in eternal shame, death eternal honor.

Since the Japanese believed firmly that they had been commanded by heaven to subjugate all people of the earth under Japanese rule, they reserved a place of great honor among the spirits for all those who died in battle. Slain soldiers became warrior gods enshrined in the Sacred Temple. Even the emperor would come to this Temple and bow in homage to the warrior gods. Each deceased soldier's name was inscribed in the Temple. Mother's received news of their son's deaths without tears knowing that their sons were now honored as warrior gods and now were spirits to guide and protect them in life. Therefore, Japanese soldiers would rather be killed than surrender.

Hirohito was told the war with the U.S. would take a few months. How the Japanese intended to defeat the powerful U.S. was, apparently, never fully thought through. At that time, the U.S. annually produced 12 times the steel, 5 times the ships, 105 times the automobiles, and 5½ times the amount of electricity than Japan.

The Japanese, however, had a secret weapon. They had *yamato damashii*, the "spirit of the warrior." Seeing Americans as merchants, the Japanese didn't believe they could carry out a long and protracted and *unprofitable* war whereas they believed they could. It was this "secret ingredient" that led the Japanese, just 1½ hours before striking Pearl Harbor, to land 20,000 troops on the east coast of Malaya to fight 88,000 Brits. The Brits soon surrendered to the Japanese. Other Japanese invasions occurred simultaneously with the Pearl Harbor invasion.

In *American Caesar*, page 323, MacArthur is quoted:

> The Japanese are the greatest exploiters of inefficient and incompetent troops the world has ever seen... Never let the Jap attack you. When the Japanese soldier has a coordinated plan of attack he works smoothly. When he is attacked - when he doesn't know what is coming - it isn't the same.

The book continues:

> Then the Nipponese were vulnerable because of their very rigidity. Their inability to imagine that they might be vanquished prevented them from planning to cope with such crises.

And so, these were the soldiers, the nation, and the mindset of Paul's enemy. They too would discover that the Americans would prove a formidable foe. Meanwhile, the Japs had driven the Aussies down the Kokoda trail to within 32 miles of Port Moresby. Though the 32nd wasn't ready, there were no divisions available to send to New Guinea to help the Australians fight back the Japanese. On September 13, 1942, MacArthur announced he was sending units of the 32nd Division to New Guinea, specifically Paul's 126th Infantry Regiment under Colonel Lawrence Quinn and the 128th Infantry regiment under Colonel Tracy Hale.

Chapter 7

New Guinea

At dawn on Tuesday, September 15, some of the 32nd flew to Port Moresby. Three days later, Paul disembarked for Port Moresby on a Liberty ship out of Rockhampton[26], 370 miles north of Brisbane. While Paul was pulling out of Rockhampton Harbor, a grass fire spread to the central dump in Port Moresby sending up a thick black cloud and detonating bombs and ammunition. Large quantities of bombs, fuses, fins, arming wires, and large amounts of ammunition were destroyed that day.

Apprehensions soared as the men boarded their Liberty ships for Port Moresby. A few weeks earlier, Cable was killed when the Japanese torpedoed his Liberty ship off the coast of Australia. No

Liberty Ship

lights or cigarettes were allowed at night on board. You would go to the brig if you did. They experienced severe weather on the way to Port Moresby. A dingy, strapped to one of the Liberty ships, blew off the ship with three men sleeping inside. They had to be retrieved the next day. One Libertyship was the *SS Holland,* another the *SS Benjamin Franklin.* Even though they had strict orders not to smoke or go on deck, when they got to Port Moresby on September 4, the dock was all lit up, Japanese bombers were flying overhead and Japanese troops were within 30 miles of Port Moresby. The men disembarked into chest high water and were told to take cover. They were taken in trucks 10-15 miles away and dropped off in the jungle and ordered to dig foxholes. Japanese bombers dropped bombs the first night and fighter planes strafed the staging area resulting in the first casualties the 32nd suffered in New Guinea. Dysentery struck the 32nd immediately. It was a rude awakening for what, up until then, had been a piece of cake in their military experience, relative to what they were about to experience in the days ahead.

Bootless Bay, Port Moresby, 1942

Bootless Bay, Port Moresby, Today

Unloading Supplies at Dock in Port Morseby

There were only three miles between the port and the mountains which made it difficult to train the soldiers, there simply was not enough room for maneuvering. The men tried to become acclimatized to the weather (one of the wettest in the world) and went on patrols during the short time they stayed in Port Moresby.

While in New Guinea, Paul loved getting mail and corresponding with folks back home. Writing and receiving letters were bigger back then. Bernice Chezlak said:

> When he was overseas and while I was in high school, I wrote him 2-3 letters a week. He would write back and sent pictures. He was so eager to get mail. In those days, people were eager to receive mail. I gave all his letters and photographs to Grandma Cavanaugh, but they were destroyed in the house explosion. The last letter I received from Paul was on 4-ply toilet paper. He said, 'I guarantee this is first-hand toilet paper, but if supplies don't get here soon, the next letter I send will be on second-hand toilet paper'.
>
> — Bernice Chezlak (1st Cousin)

Marcella related:

> I sent him a box of cookies once and received a letter back from him saying not to send anything else

because the weather was damp, the jungle so thick
that food was bad by the time he got it... Paul had a
girlfriend in Carroll. I think he would have married
her and gone into farming with Dad if he returned
from the military.

— Marcela Judson (sister)

Natives would come into camp out of curiosity. The GI's called
them "Gooks" or "Fuzzy Wuzzies." One man reported seeing a
woman nursing her child with one breast and feeding a pig with the
other. They loved shinny objects. Melody said you could buy a village
for a quarter but your dollar bills were worth nothing.

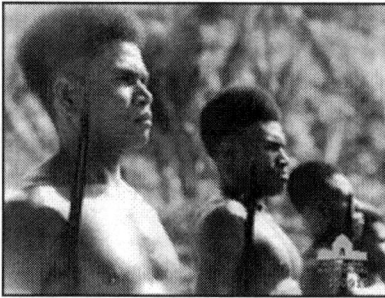

"Gooks" or "Fuzzy Wuzzies" received
pay to help in the war effort.

Natives helped carry the wounded.

The natives had large gardens with yams and other vegetables.
Soldiers were told not to take anything or the natives would embellish
and exaggerate what was taken. Natives filled long sticks of bamboo
with edibles including leaves and fish heads and cooked them. When
the bamboo sticks were cooked, they cut them open and their
contents were eaten.

The Army recruited the Gooks from their villages. 65 came from
Natunga, for example, and were paid to help carry supplies, the
wounded, and serve as scouts (one scout could smell the Japs). Many
Gooks had yet to align with one side or the other. They wanted to see

who was winning and who treated them best. Natives were given $5 for every Japanese head they brought in, but because so many heads were brought in, the natives began bringing in ears. The 32nd was warned that some natives would try to make them laugh just to see their gold fillings, a discovery some former cannibals might find tempting.

The Japanese who fought the Australians from Buna down the 130-mile Kokoda trail were emaciated and exhausted but exultant as they stood on top of Ioribaiwa Ridge looking down onto Port Moresby in the distance.

Their exuberance wasn't to last long. They received a crushing blow, not from the Allies but from their own commanders. The telegrams were clear. Their leader, Major Horii, was ordered to retreat, "Stop attacking Port Moresby, and wait for further instructions." Major Horii was beside himself. The second telegram received said, "Withdraw from present position to some point in the Owen Stanley Range which you consider best for strategic purposes." Horii might have ignored these two commands until the third came from the Emperor himself, "... withdraw completely from the Owen Stanley's and concentrate on the coast at Buna." In response to this order, one Japanese soldier's diary entry wrote of a "terrible grief" that "cut deep into our hearts." Japan had decided to focus their efforts on Guadalcanal and withdrew from the soon-to-be-conquered, Port Morseby.

On Friday, September 18, Paul's company flew over the Owen Stanley Mountains in a one-hour flight to Pongani, possibly the first-time Paul flew in an airplane. Nearly two weeks later, on Monday, October 5, 1942, Dad was inducted into the military in Des Moines, driving there with Mom, Grandpa, Grandma, and Marilyn. Dad would serve in the Army Air Corp as a bomber pilot. Paul was killed two months to the day of Dad's induction.

While Paul made his journey through the Hydrographer Mountains, the Australians began bombarding the Japanese, Port Morseby stronghold of Ioribaiwa Ridge on September 25. The Japanese withdrawal to Gona began on September 26. Horii had hoped the Japanese would secure Guadalcanal so forces could be diverted to New Guinea for their conquest of the country, but it was not to be.

On October 3, the Australian counteroffensive began in earnest as the Japanese fell into full retreat for the Gona-Sanananda-Buna beachhead on the northern coast. 3,000 Japanese engineers had already prepared a nearly impregnable defense system.

MacArthur flew in from Brisbane for the occasion. He was in New Guinea about a day and with the troops one hour. After McArthur's pep talk, the Aussie's 16th Brigade began their fight up the Kokoda Trail toward the northern shores of Gona-Sanananda-Buna retracing the very path they were driven down.

This Australian counteroffensive would ultimately put the Aussies in position to attack Gona, the western most city of the Japanese, three-city beachhead (Gona-Sanananda-Buna). They would serve as one prong of a three-prong attack by the Allies. While the Aussie 16th Brigade advanced back up the Kokoda trail toward Gona, Paul's 126th Regiment of the 3rd Battalion, which constituted the second of the three-prong, "Buna" attack, would fly from Port Moresby to Pongani and march on the Pongani-Popondette trail through the Hydrographer's Mountain Range through Natunga, Bofu, Popondetta, and to Soputa along the western side of the Girua River and east of the Aussie 16th Brigade.

Meanwhile, the 2nd Battalion or the Ghost Mountain Boys led by Major Stutterin' Smith, advanced into position to support the Sanananda attack. They had been transported from Port Moresby to a coastal village about 40 miles south of Port Moresby called Kapa Kapa. The soldiers mispronounced the town as Gaba Gaba. They then advanced up a trail to Kalikadobu, a town the 2nd Battalion affectionately nicknamed "Kalamazoo" (in honor of their native Michigan). The 2nd Battalion then marched across the entire country over the Owen Stanley Mountains to Jaure. From Jaure Major Stutterin' Smith's "Ghost Mountain Boys" continued their march toward the village of Sanananda where they intended to link-up with Paul's group, the 3rd Battalion, 126th Infantry unit at Soputa, a village south of Sanananda.

There was a change in plans, however. Instead of joining Paul's unit in an attack against Sanananda, and although already in position to do so, the 2nd Battalion was diverted to the opposite or eastern side of the Girua river to support the 128th in the third of a three-prong offensive against the Japanese at Buna. The 128th flew into the northern coastal village of Wanigela, over 100 miles east of Buna. They marched along the coast approaching Buna from the east.

So, the first prong of the attack was the Aussies up the Kokoda Trail to Gona; the second prong was the 3rd Battalion's 126th marching from Pongani on the Pongani-Popondette trail and north to Soputa for an attack against Sanananda, and the third prong was a combined, "pincher attack" force against Buna of the 128th coming from the east along the coast and the 2nd Battalion from the south.

By November 16 the northward assault up the Kokoda Trail brought the Australians to the Kumusi River at Wairopi where they prepared for the march on Gona. On November 19 at 0700, the Australians attacked the well-fortified, Japanese stronghold of Gona. On November 20, the 126th reached Soputa. They were given some of the 21st off as a day of rest in preparation for advancing against Sanananda on the 22nd. They staged themselves on the west side of the Girua with 1,400 men.

Paul fought with Australian soldiers who had been in Syria, Libya, Crete, and Egypt and then went straight to New Guinea without going home first. All the vets I interviewed agreed on how tough the Aussies were. Where the Australians would make a fire and boil water for the daily tea, the Americans saw that as a death wish by potentially giving away their position. The Aussies seemed to have a "devil may care," attitude. Because they didn't seem to care about the noise they were making to produce a "spot of tea," many Americans tried to avoid the Aussies. The Australians were great at using their bayonet. If there was a machine gun nest, according to one GI, the Aussies would rush it with 20 men and if they took over the nest, regardless of loss of life, it was a victory.

Van Hammen told me that a young man whose dad was killed in the Buna campaign contacted him. The man only had one photo of his father. One day he was showing a picture of his father to someone who identified the uniform worn by his father as an Australian uniform and said the photo couldn't be of his father. This young man flew to Grand Rapids to meet some of the 32nd and talked with Van Hammen who looked at the picture and said that it wasn't uncommon for some Americans to end up in an Aussie uniform and that the photo was indeed of his father.

Chapter 8

To The Front

On Tuesday, November 10, 1942, Paul was flown from an airstrip outside of Port Moresby to Pongani's makeshift runway on the northern shores of New Guinea. He was being sent to the front. Edwin Wesholski's diary entry on that day said:

> Fell in on road with full equipment (0945); loaded on trucks (1043); departed from Bootless Bay (1059); arrived at airport (Ward's Drome[27], 1126); took off at 1153.

Gooks had chopped down Kunai grass to make the Pongani runway smooth enough for a landing. Perhaps a few days before Paul took off, the 126th attended the memorial service for their first leader, Colonel Quinn, who died in a plane crash on November 5.

Each plane was assigned an officer. Care was given to make sure that the different MOS's were assigned to different airplanes so if any went down, they wouldn't lose all of one skill set. The airplanes all left within one or two hours of one another. One Grand Rapids vet told me that he had a buddy that wanted to fly with him. Since their larger platoon was divided between two aircraft, the *Flying Dutchman* and the *Golden Eight Ball*, he and his buddy flipped to see who would go on which of the two planes. Fortunately for him, he drew the *Golden Eight Ball*.

As the *Flying Dutchman* flew over the Owen Stanley Mountains with a crew of 23, a strong down draft plunged the aircraft into the 9,000' Mount Obree. Six men died on impact. Of the remaining seventeen, eight were seriously injured and eight were well enough to break into two teams of four to go for help. One left behind was able to retrieve water for the other eight injured soldiers who remained with the aircraft. One team of four left on November 12 and another on the 16th. Two of these eight would die seeking help, the other six survived and secured help on December 14, 32 days after they left the crash site. After eight days of searching over the ground, however, and despite aerial reconnaissance efforts, no trace of the aircraft was found. The last diary entry at the site was posted on January 1, 1943. These daily entries were inscribed on the airplane door and found when the crash was discovered in July of 1944. The eight wounded men were all found dead.

The entries written on the door were in two columns:

Daily Entries on Door:
(Left Column)

Crashed 1:30 Tues - 10 of Nov. — 1942

Tues-10, 17 men alive

Wed-11, 16 men alive

Thurs-12, 4 men started for help

Fri-13

Sat-14, Tried to put up balloon

Sun-15, Cracker and cheese

Mon-16, 4 men started for help-due South leaves eight men left

Tues-17, Small piece cheese

Wed-18, Chocolate bar

Thurs-19, Found one chocolate bar

Fri-20, 1/3 can tomato juice

Sat-21, 1/3 can tomato juice

Sun-22, Drank last 1/3 can of tomato juice

Mon-23, Last cigarette-even butts

Tues-24, First day-no rain

Wed-25, 2nd day-no rain

Thurs-26, Rain today-also clear in morning

Fri-27, Bucket full water this morn-still got our chin up

Sat-28, Clearest day we have had

Sun-29, Nice clear day. Boy we're getting weak still have our hope

Mon-30, Still going strong on imaginary meals

December Tues-1, My summer is here - went to spring today

Wed-2, Just slid by but boy it rained

Thurs-3, Kinda cold and cloudy today-still plenty hungry-boy a cig. would do good

Fri-4, Same ole thing-clear this morn

Sat-5, Boy nothing happened-just waiting

Sun-6, Had service today. Still lots of hope

Mon-7, Year ago today the war started. Boy we didn't think of this then

Tues-8, Nice day - still living on thru this

Wed-9, Cloudy. God is looking out for our water supply

Thurs-10, Just thirty days ago. We can take it but would be nice if someone came

(Right Column)

Fri-11, Cold rainy day. We would like to start out before Christmas

Sat-12, Fairly nice day-still plenty of water

Sun-13, Beautiful morning everyone has high hopes

Mon-14, Waiting

Tues-15, Waiting

Wed-16, New water place today

Thurs-17, Running out of imaginary meals. Boys shouldn't be long in coming now. Six more shopping days

Fri-18, Nice and warm this morning. Rained in the afternoon

Sat-19, Pretty cold last night. Cold this morning too. Water pretty low. Five more days till Xmas

Sun-20

Mon-21, Plenty of water

Tues-22, Rained all three days

Wed-23, Thinking about home and Christmas. Still hoping

Thurs-24, Tonight is Christmas Eve. God make them happy at home

Fri-25, Christmas Day

Sat-26

Sun-27, Rain every day

Mon-28

Tues-29

Wed-30, Johnnie died today

Thurs-31

Fri-1, New Year's Day

Pat

Mart

Ted

(on lower left of door)

    Except for the *Flying Dutchman*, the men arrived at about 1430 on November 10 at the Pongani airfield which was in a meadow outside of Pongani. After disembarking from their aircraft, they assembled for their advance to Sanananda, leaving at 1535. Their 12-day journey began on the Pongani-Natunga trail. The men were issued 3-days of rations and given C-rations which included one can each of hash, beans, and stew; and a new pair of socks with one sock ½-full of rice. Rice was difficult to cook since wood was soaking wet and a fire could give your position away, although they were less concerned about that through the Hydrographer's Mountain Range since they didn't expect many Japanese in that area. They journeyed single file and reached that night's bivouac area at 1642. Their journey would take them through Natunga, Bofu, and Popondette before they reached Soputa. Their mission was to attack the Japanese at Sanananda Point just a few miles north of Soputa. One soldier commented, "We didn't know the names of these villages, we might have heard the names but would probably forget them."

Wesholski continued:

> Nov. 11/42 (Day Two), Reveille at 0500; 5-7 ate individual rations and prepared to leave; 0740-1215, standing by for Lt. Evans and remainder of company; 0945, War correspondent, F. C. Widdis, A. P. attached; 1109, Major Bond, Capt. Huggins, Sgt. Foster, PFC Cowell, Pvt. Kalled, Sojourner FCH. Smith & war correspondent Widdis went ahead; 1400, departed from bivouac area; 1630 reached new bivouac area about 5 miles from old area.

According to Wesholski, they reached their bivouac area at "some river" on November 12 (Day Three) at 1530 and spent time cleaning their clothes and themselves before going to bed. The men spent 0700 – 0830 on November 14 (Day Four) cleaning their rifles and left their bivouac area at 0840. At 1415, they reached their first ration dump at the village of Natunga. Platoon leaders secured 3-days of rations and distributed them to their men. Their next ration dump was on November 17 (Day Seven), the day Robert Cavanaugh was killed in Great Britain. They passed a ration dump but did not stop on November 18. They reached their new bivouac area at 1410 on November 18 (Day Eight) where they gathered with the rest of their battalion (this became a staging area for the offensive).

In fear of the impending crisis, many of the villagers evacuated their homes leaving the villages empty as the soldiers marched through. The soldiers marched down the two-feet wide, Popondetta trail single file. "You just followed the guy ahead of you." Some of the wildlife was beautiful, especially birds like Macaws and Cockatoos.

The Hydrographer's Mountain range presented itself as a formidable obstacle to negotiate. These mountains are extremely steep; in fact, the soldiers would have to dig in their heels to take naps in order not to slide down the mountainsides. The rain and mud was constant. They marched fifty minutes, rested ten, and slept wherever they could find a level place, not an easy task in the dark. Some attempted to light fires along the way for hot cups of coffee. There were no Japanese in that portion of their journey but again, finding dry wood was not easy. The soldiers crossed several rivers and almost lost several men in the crossings. One soldier remembered one guy that no one liked almost being swept away before a fellow soldier could grab him. The other soldiers complained, "Why didn't you let the SOB go"?

There was water everywhere, constantly, and everything was wet. The men were issued "shelter halves," a canvas with buttons that the men could roll into or drape over themselves to keep warm during the cooler nights. Two men could put their halves together and make a pump tent. Ponchos were used more than anything and even giant banana leaves (often used by Fuzzy Wuzzies to shade the wounded from the sun). The jungle was so thick it was difficult at times to know if the sun was shining or not.

Planes were scheduled for three separate supply drops along the way, but none of them could be located in the thick jungle. Melody lost 65 pounds in three months. The food was gone by the time they got to the roadblock, Paul's final battle.

The days were extremely hot. Many of the soldiers threw away what they didn't think they would need. Leggings, the first to go, were cut off into shorts; razors thrown away; mosquito bars tossed; even helmets, rifles, and pistols were discarded along the way.

Some needed supplies were replaced when they drew closer to Soputa. One veteran of the Buna campaign said:

> Some soldiers threw away their helmets. I threw mine away but kept the liner. Those were good helmets, great for getting water for bathing. We didn't need to wear helmets all the time since there wasn't a lot of artillery like there was in the Philippines where you had to wear them. You had to be there. It's hard to explain otherwise.

The soldiers came upon downed Zeros; water-filled bomb craters which made for great baths; and occasionally, delectable goats stumbled across their path. One vet I spoke with caught a chicken and ate it raw. He became very ill. As one man said, "The march from Pongani to Soputa doesn't look far on the map, but I thought we'd never get there."

As the soldiers made their way to Soputa, the Japanese knew they were "out there somewhere." One vet said, "Tokyo Rose[28] warned us of Jap airplanes and, sure enough, they came." The men were told not to build fires and to take care in not giving away their position. One day, enough was enough, a Japanese Zero had harassed the men several days while it searched for them on the mountainside. One GI couldn't take it any longer. When he had a clear shot at the Zero scout, he fired one round. The bullet apparently hit a gas line causing the plane to plummet in flames. One of the Michigan men of the 32nd said, "You thought you were at a U of M football game when you heard the guys cheering.

It was as the men descended the mountains in their approach to Soputa, that they heard rifle shots and machine gun fire. "That's when it all got real," one vet said.

As the men drew closer to Soputa, an airlift of supplies was retrieved. Included in the supplies was "bully beef" a disgusting meat (beef or mutton) that caused the men to gag. A lot of the corn beef dropped was putrid. The men were told to eat the WWI rations down to where they turned green and then to toss it. There were no fruit trees in the area; they had been cut down ... not with machetes but with machine gun fire. Some men were already getting malaria, dengue fever, and diarrhea.

Weshlowski continued:

> November 20 (Day Ten), reveille at 0700 a.m.; 1530 ordered to move on. Comm PLT rejoined CO. Reiff evacuated to 107 Med. One day rations issued. Maj Zeff & Mindykowski rejoined Co.; 1610 Co moved out. Widrig, Watson, Gedreis; 2045 reached bivouac area near Australian troops – Poppendetta.

They reached Soputa and a ration dump on November 21 (Day Eleven) at 1230 p.m. and set up their camp area. One day's ration was issued. Weshlowski wrote, "1900, Att. I Co men rejoined own outfit. Lt. Woltjer assgd to Reg. VOCO; large quantities of rations issued. Widrig, Gedris, Watson on supply detail." They were there one day and as one vet related, "We killed some Japs and some Japs killed some of our men." Moral was very high until men began to see their friends killed. The 32nd had a policy not to take prisoners because it took five men to watch one prisoner. In hand-to-hand combat situations, our men were instructed to cut the Jap's throat deep enough so they couldn't scream.

The soldiers were told to take the rest of the day off in preparation for the 22nd offensive (Day Twelve). The first thing they did was to dig their foxholes. After that, Smested set about setting up the switchboard for phone communication. Smested said there were radios, Morse Code radios, and telephones in the battle zones. Radios often didn't work as well because their batteries ran down and the jungle moisture ruined their effectiveness. Telephone reception was best but the Japanese would often cut the lines Smested laid. From time to time, Smested would have to find the breaks and fix them. He would always take two riflemen with him so they could stand guard while he gave attention to repairing the break.

Bivouac at Soputa, New Guinea

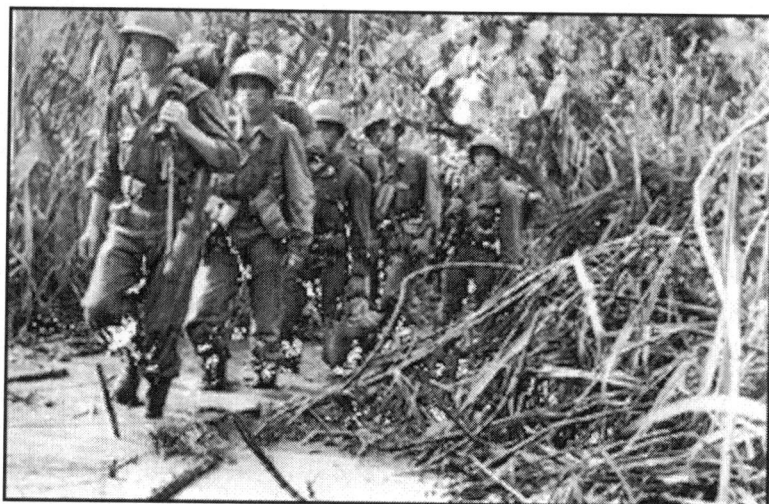

Soldiers outside of Soputa, New Guinea.

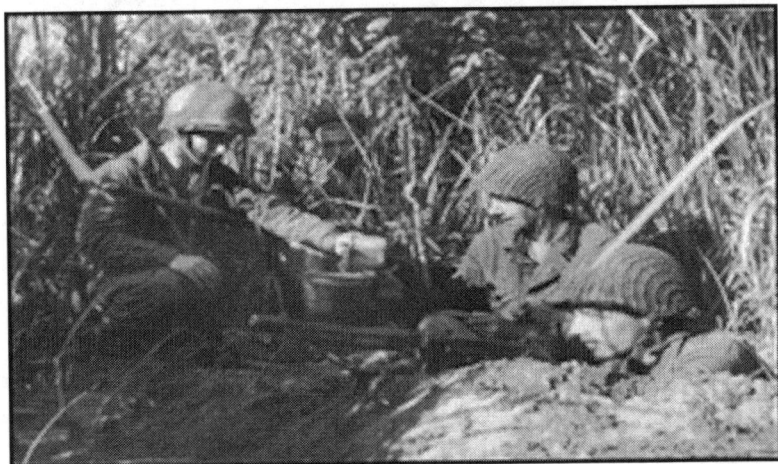

American GI's near Soputa, New Guinea.

On November 22, the men advanced from Soputa north toward Sanananda on the Sanananda trail. Their faces were smeared in green. Weshlowski writes:

> Nov. 22, Reveille at 0330; 0600 departed for the front, Lt. Kanapale made Comm. Officer. Chaplain Dzienis and Pfeiffer att. To HQ Co; 0818, HQ Co C. P. established; 1250, C. P. advanced; 1300, New C.P. established 150 yards ahead.

Father Stephen Dzienis

They entered the swamp west and east of the Sanananda trail. No one felt cocky at this point. They respected the enemy they faced even though the Japanese were fighting under worse conditions than the Americans and Australians.

Faced off in an unmovable front, most of the last week of November was spent trying to establish a roadblock behind enemy lines on the Sanananda track. Swamp water was up to their knees or chest for about three or four days. The men scared most of the animals away, slept where they could, had no place to stop to prepare food, ate some C-rations, drank swamp water by putting chlorine tablets in canteens, and started running into Japs in the swamps. Many men, sick with malaria, took daily quinine tablets. Rumor had it, however, that the pills could make one sterile, a deterrent to some of the men. Fevers had to reach 104 degrees for the men to be pulled out of combat. Weshlowski records:

Nov. 25: Patrol sent to establish forward CP (command post) and communications with I and K, Maj. Bond, Capt Huggins, Lt. Gibbs, Lt. Kanapaux, G. Carpenter, Sgt Baron, Corp/t Allen, Sgt. Kramarz, Smestad, Doty, Wesholski, Shaffer, Sgt. Rector, Shirley, Kinney, Cpt. McCarthy, Guild, Cowell, Buckhannon, Cpt. Rodriguez., Spellman, Mondorf, Mays, Moses, Stoard, Frederick, Streit, Cpt. Gray, Sgt Osse, Med. Brigg. **Buckhannon killed Jap officer;** 1700, Stretcher party to L Co; 1830, stretcher party to L. Co; 2200. Major Zeef in command of L. Co. Lt Powell, Shearer, Murray, Sheef, Skyee, B. Wilson attached to L. Co.

The front was all around them. The soldiers knew they had to keep looking for the enemy, kill them, and continue pushing forward. Thanksgiving was on November 26.

One vet commented:

When we walked into a clearing into the jungle, all hell broke out. The jungle was so thick that it was hard to see 4' in front of you. You could step over a log and drop into a mud pit up to your armpits. Holding your rifle up over your head, you wondered how you're going to get out of there. Every morning, we got morning reports telling us who got killed and from what unit and that sort of thing.

"There was a difference between the GI rifle and the Japanese rifles. Their rifles had a snap and ours a hard bang." The standard Japanese infantry weapon was the Arisaka Model 38 rifle. It was heavy and long but made a good jungle weapon. Its awkward length meant that the muzzle did not flash when fired as did the American M-1. The Japanese also had a smokeless powder that helped conceal the shooter's position. The Arisaka used a .25-round, the same used by Japanese machine guns, making resupply easier. One vet mentioned that the Japs also set off fireworks to incite fear.

Chaplains, Protestant and Catholic, conducted burial services.

Father Dzienis was Catholic chaplain for the 126th. He conducted masses and served as a spiritual guide to the Catholics especially. He was a front-line pastor that earned the respect of all the soldiers. One night, late in November and on the Sanananda front, he was utilizing a recently dug, two-hole outhouse when the Japanese navy bombed their camp. He ran out of the outhouse with his pants down around his ankles, yelling, "To hell with the Geneva Convention, give me a pistol"!

> 37-year-old Lieutenant Stephen Dzienis went to the front on the Soputa-Sanananda track Nov. 22. He said at least one mass every day, besides giving absolution, anointing the wounded, and burying the dead. The first soldier he buried was a Jew. He read from a Jewish prayer book and erected a Star of David with sticks over the grave. Once Father Dzienis started a mass for 70 Americans and Australians near the front at 10:30 a.m. At 10:45 the Japs began dropping shells. No one moved until the mass was completed and the men had said the prayer: "Holy Michael, the archangel, defend us in battle..." Then all dived for cover.

Father Dzienis moved from unit to unit carrying a small altar stone, altar linens, and communion bread in a metal can. He handed out communion nearly 800 times on the front. The soldiers crawled back one or two at a time from their foxholes to take communion at the makeshift altar. Father Dzienis was evacuated due to disease on December 28.

One emotional challenge the soldiers all had was time and distance from family. There was no way to tell their families where they were. Their families only knew their loved one was "somewhere in the South Pacific." It was difficult for families too. They would read of various battles throughout the South Pacific but not know which battle their loved one was in. Weshlowski continued:

Nov. 26 Thanksgiving

0840 Men attached to HQ Co. S/Sgt Ketchell, Pvts, Ryon, Peterson, Weirgowski, Pixley, Fomin from Reg. HQ Co

1100 Sgt Kotecki and 21 men sent to guard L. Co rear and flank

1330 Sgts Foley, Augur, Pvts Johnson, Sandstrom, Butler with Reg. HQ Co

NOT IN DIARY: **Merle Holm** of Lake City was killed in action.

Nov. 27 Men attached to M Co carrying rations to I & K. Pvt Myers reports to rear S-4 ER Base.

PFC Buckhannon Killed in Action (See November 25)

0930 Ney and Drollinger attchd to 1st BN. Sgt Oossee returned to Co. Cpl/T Murray – D – wounded by motar fire.

0800 Remainder of HQ Co attached to M Co. Men attached to M. Co on ration and ammo carrying parties.

Nov. 28 Men attached to M Co – carrying rations to I & K & L Co

Nov. 29 Men attached to Co M, carrying rations to I & K & L Co

Nov. 30 Major Bond wounded by mortar fire – on Dc w/I & K Co.; Lt. Powell goes to hospital – chest – nervous condition; Cpl Rodriguez goes to hosp – SK

NOT IN DIARY: Co I attacked Japanese position and secured roadblock

Dec. 1   Ration parties to I - K - L Cos.
          NOT IN DIARY: Keast killed in action on roadblock

Dec. 2   PFC Fierst - wounded - Pvt Conrad wounded & shock - Pvt Smith sk in hosp. Pvt Blair - sk in hosp - Pvt Sandstrom - sk in hosp - ration parties to I & K Co

          NOT IN DIARY: Shirley killed in action on roadblock next to Edgington (and Paul?)

Dec. 3   Thursday. Major Zeeff - 4 wire men. G. Henning return w/ Co L

Dec. 4   Friday. PFC Guild returns to "I & K" Co

Dec. 5   Saturday. 3rd HQ Co activated VOCO; PFC Towne goes to hosp - sk, Pvt Rowely returns Fr Co "L." Johnson det. Pvt Rowely sk in hosp - Fever

          NOT IN DIARY: Paul Cavanaugh killed in action; Captain Huggins wounded by sniper.

Dec. 6   Pvt Johnson, Pvt Lanning, Cpl Michalak all sick in hosp with fever; Sgt Simons & 10 EM return from defense guard HQ Co to rest area; Lt. Sikkel, Pvt Stevenson, PFC White go to "I & K" Co on ration party, have not returned as of this date.

Dec. 7   3 HQ Co EM order forward as rear guard for Aussie attack.; Cpl. Grubba, Pvt Skyee, Pvt P. Wilson sk in hosp - fever; Cpl Jack White - wounded by sniper fire - sent to hosp; Lt. Sikkell, Pvt Stevenson - PFC White still missing w/ration party.

Dec. 8   Lt. Sikkell, Pvt Stevenson, PFC White return Fr ration party to "I & K" Cos. Capt Huggins returns Fr Co "I" w/head wounded. Was wounded on Dec. 5. S/Sgt Kotecki – returns Fr Co "I" sk w/fever; S/Sgt Simons – returns Fr front line defense – sk w/fever; Pvt Tobin returns Fr "I & K" w/fever. Weshlowski's journal continued until January 29, 1943.

Chapter 9

The Roadblock

Our biggest battle was Huggins Roadblock, that is
where I was lucky and made it. God willing. That is
where we were pinned down for four weeks. No tent,
no food, muddy water to drink. Hand grenades flying
and bullets. If you got out of the foxhole you were
dead.

The 126th was up against 4,000 well-trained and experienced
Japanese soldiers and was surprised to find many well-fed,
healthy enemy troops among those slain. In recent days, nearly 1,000
new Japanese reinforcements had, unknowingly to the Americans,
arrived in Sanananda port and descended the Sanananda trail to the
front.

The Japanese on the Gona front, however, had fought their way
back to Gona from Port Moresby and were beat down and starving.
They were in worse condition than either the Aussies or the
Americans. The Japanese being pushed back on the Kokoda trail,
resorted to cannibalism, first eating Australian dead (cutting off pieces
of meat little by little since there was no refrigeration) and eventually
eating their own dead. Major Mitsuo Moiwai of 2nd Battalion 41st
Infantry commented after the war, "We were in such a position we
wondered whether the Americans would bypass us and let us starve."
Some believe that that's exactly what MacArthur should have done
and as the War progressed did do through his strategy of island
hopping.

On the Sanananda front, a few miles north of Soputa, little
headway was being made and the Japs had a continual flow of recruits

and supplies down the Sanananda trail to their front lines. The Allies decided to establish a roadblock behind the front in order to cut off supplies from Sanananda and Buna (there were no supplies or soldiers from Gona). The last week of November was spent trying to get into position to establish the roadblock behind enemy lines on the Sanananda track.

Companies I and K were initially ordered to flank left, positioning themselves west of the enemy and Company L was to flank right. Companies I and K advanced nearly 350 yards against Japanese resistance; Company L, 200 yards. The next few days the Americans attempted to improve their positions in preparation for a new attack.

A patrol was sent out every day to gather information and usually there was at least one casualty. Reports were given each morning sharing casualty losses. None of the vets I interviewed remembered Paul but they did say they would have been told of his death. Passwords were issued to the men as they left, but if they were gone too long, it was possible the password would have changed and your own soldiers might shoot you. In fact, one soldier accidentally killed his buddy because of a changed password. Passwords usually had the letter "R" in them: Ruth, Robin, etc. because the Japs had a hard time pronouncing "R." Finally, one patrol discovered a weakness between two Japanese positions that could potentially serve as an inroad to establishing the roadblock.

On November 26, Thanksgiving Day, K and I gained better positions paying dearly with the loss of good soldiers such as Merle Holm of Lake City (Company K). Paul would be killed nine days later. During Paul's days in New Guinea, Bernice sent several letters a week to Paul and received many letters and photographs from him. Unfortunately, they were all destroyed when Grandpa's and Grandma's home burned down. I asked Bernice if she had any recollection of the content of Paul's letters. She only remembers Paul saying he was afraid he wasn't coming home.

On November 29, Company I and Company K (under Major Baetcke), parts of Company M, the canon company, and the antitank company (under Keast), were all led by Captain John Shirley in successfully positioning themselves to reach the main trail behind the Japanese position. It was a breakthrough. They scheduled an attack to secure the roadblock for the next day, November 30. The Ghost Mountain Boys had the toughest terrain issues. Company I had their share of terrain issues as well, but those on the roadblock experienced the worse the enemy had to throw at them for four weeks.

Since there were no enemy tanks, the antitank company became infantrymen. All toll, there were about 635 men on the roadblock. Of these men, only 175 would walk out alive several weeks later.

On November 30, Company I advanced to a swamp protected by a Japanese machine gun nest. Shirley assembled a patrol of ten men who got within thirty feet of the machine gun nest, threw in a grenade, and knocked it out. Uncle Paul may have been one of those ten men especially given the fact that Paul, Edgington, and Shirley were next to one another on the roadblock, according to Edgington's letter to Marcella.

With the machine gun nest taken out, Shirley and Keast saw their opportunity to drive through the Japanese line with the Japanese in full retreat. They situated themselves in a clearing that would soon be referred to as, the Roadblock, later named the Huggin's Roadblock. They decided to rest their troops. The Roadblock was firmly established by 6:30 p.m. on November 30. The men held up against two Japanese counterattacks that evening. The Roadblock was 1500 yards behind enemy lines, an oval shaped clearing roughly 150 yards wide and 300 yards long with the Sanananda road dissecting the oval-shaped perimeter. Tin cans with stones placed in them, were attached to wires strung across the road to alert our soldiers to unsuspecting Japanese soldiers walking down its path. Sometimes our men would hear the cans or their tossed C-ration cans clanking in the middle of the night only to be relieved that it was a rat.

Shirley's scouts located an enemy stronghold later that evening. Shirley and Keast decided to attack before nightfall and divided the men into three platoons. Shirley ordered bayonets fixed and told the men to attack on the signal of two shots. The order was passed down the line. Shirley and Keast led the charge. "Fix your bayonets and let's cut the guts out of them," Shirley cried as he fired two shots. Fauna ripped at the men's legs as they ran through the jungle not knowing where the Japs were. Some heard the thump of bullets entering human flesh of a soldier next to them. Suddenly, they ran into a solid mass of enemy soldiers. Men fired at point-blank range and slashed and lunged with their bayonets. Blood splattered everywhere. Hand-to-hand combat ensued. Shirley strangled a Japanese soldier as he felt his body thrashing under his hands.

The Roadblock was secured and the men dug in! Wounded could be heard crying out, the intense heat bloated corpses, the stench of human flesh was present as a breeze came in from the ocean cooling the jungle.

Earlier on, some Japs walked down the road not aware they were walking through the Roadblock. One vet told me, "We picked them off like rabbits at first. Some of them didn't even have rifles because they were behind their own front lines."[29]

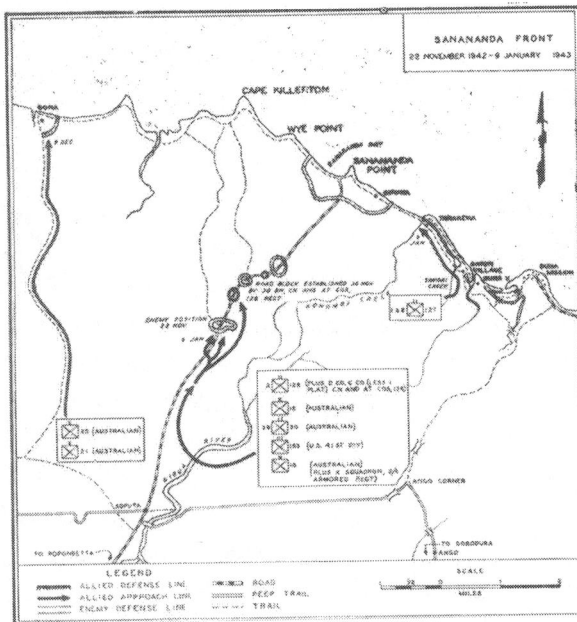

Diagram of Sanananda Assault and Roadblock

It was only after the Road-block was established that the soldiers realized how precarious their situation was. They were one mile behind enemy lines knowing the Japanese would soon be sending more troops from Sanananda-Buna to attack the Roadblock from the north, literally surrounding the men on the Roadblock. With Jap snipers soon strapped into the trees around the Roadblock, the men on the Roadblock were easy targets for the snipers firing with smokeless rifles.

Snipers killed many Americans but there were good shots among the Americans as well. One vet I interviewed reported that a fellow GI from "out west" was a great shot and killed 32 Japs while on the Roadblock. Paul also was a good shot (at least when it came to pheasants).

More battles ensued. The GI's repelled assault after assault. Huggins called their situation chaotic. One stretch of Japanese attack lasted for nearly 1½ days non-stop. The GI's put up panels for American bombers to see their position and removed them when enemy planes flew overhead.

The Roadblock was almost impossible to defend on December 1. Keast suggested he lead an information gathering patrol off the southwest corner of the perimeter. Shirley reluctantly agreed to what led to Keast's death a few hours later. One of the men in the patrol was left wounded and hid amidst enemy soldiers for several days before being found by Americans.

The Japanese attacked the Roadblock again on December 2 and succeeded in reducing its

Major Meredith Huggins

perimeter but not in breaking through. At one point in the battle, Shirley needed the phone. He yelled to Smested for it, but Smested said his assistant dropped the phone earlier when they were under fire and pinned down. Shirley ordered them to go back and get it.

Smested remembers Shirley asking a soldier how he was doing after being shot in the neck. When the soldier replied, "OK," Smested heard Shirley say, "If that happened to me I'd cry like a baby."

Van Hammen remembers that he looked up and saw B-17's flying overhead just before Shirley got killed. Edgington and Smested both said they were standing next to Shirley when he was killed. Since Edgington told me he was ten yards away from Paul when Paul was killed, Paul was, undoubtedly, near Shirley also. Shirley had a gut wound and asked a buddy how bad it was. He was crying out for his mom and scribbled a note to her. Shirley was killed with an Australian lieutenant, one of the few Aussies that had been assigned to the Roadblock. The 126th generally didn't fight side-by-side with the Aussies but each relieved the other from time to time.

The Japanese signaled each other with birdcalls. When a lot of birdcalls were heard, the GI's chirped in with a few more of their own whistles, just to confuse the enemy. On one such occasion this prank caused a Japanese soldier to yell in perfect English, "Shut up, you American bastards!"

The GI's got use to the mosquitoes. Some made rookie mistakes swatting at them, giving away their position. Sometimes the GI's fired at sounds in the jungle or at movements in the brush. It was difficult to see the enemy though they were just outside the perimeter. The jungle was filled with them.

One day, a crazy Japanese soldier who had apparently lost his mind, dressed up in an American uniform and walked up to the perimeter and taunted GI's in one of the foxholes in Spanish! He then turned around and walked away when someone shot him. The kill was confirmed the next day.

Snipers were clever. There could be three snipers to cover a certain area of jungle or a certain area of a trail. They might watch you for a while and then open-up. You had to stay in the trench or you would be killed. Snipers looked for officers. Because officers didn't carry rank or insignias, the enemy looked to the ones giving orders to identify them. One sniper could hold up an entire company, even a battalion. "I never saw a sniper in a tree but saw some dangling from a tree," reported one vet. Smested said a lot of the men on the Roadblock threw their helmets away walking across the Hydrographer Mountain Range. Replacement supplies had not yet been secured for these men by December 5. For that reason, many of the men, according to Smested, were not wearing helmets. Was Uncle Paul wearing a helmet? If not, would having had his helmet had saved his life?

The Roadblock was threatened again on December 3 by unceasing Japanese assaults. Tromp, who eventually was relieved with a 105-degree temperature (three degrees above the required threshold), shared about an experience he had that was similar to Uncle Paul's.

"X" identifies the Japanese sniper that wounded Huggins the day Paul was killed. This soldier was killed and the photo was found on his body. He could have been the sniper that killed Uncle Paul.

"I went to get into my foxhole and there was a man in it. I asked what he was doing in there and he said he had been shot in the neck." Tromp said, "I know, you already told me you got shot in the neck." The soldier retorted, "Ya, and I got shot a second time, standing right where you're at."

Tromp immediately dove into the hole with his wounded comrade. Tromp continued:

> As time went on, we'd improve our foxhole, make them deeper and with more space to move around. The water table was shallow. We had water in the trenches and would drink the water in the trench even with mosquito larval swimming around.
> — Woodrow (Woody) Tromp

The battle was at a fever pitch on December 5, the sixth day of the Japanese offense to break the Roadblock. Huggins was wounded, narrowly missing death, having been shot in the head. He was bandaged up with a white bandage. Van Hammen told him to take the bandage off his head or he'd get shot again. The Roadblock was named after Major Huggins (whom I interviewed) for doing such a great job in holding it, but it was Shirley that succeeded in leading the effort to get it.

Huggins was wounded on December 5; the day Paul was killed. According to Edgington, Paul was "always getting out of his foxhole to get the Japs." Melody said he heard Paul was shot in the head as he attempted to jump into his foxhole with someone already in it.

> The news of Paul's death was the most severe blow I ever received. To this day, I can't talk about it without crying (69 years later). We were close to the same age. I loved him so much. There was nothing malignant in his character. There wasn't a mean bone in his body. He always had a good, positive word.
> — Marcella Judson, Paul's sister

Melody reflected, "God, I didn't think there were enough Japs in

New Guinea to kill Paul Cavanaugh." The *Enterprise* published an article, "Paul Cavanaugh First Lohrville War Casualty" on January 28, 1943:

> The tragedy of war struck home in the community on Monday morning when Mr. And Mrs. William Cavanaugh received a telegram that their son, Paul, had been killed in action on December 5. When last heard from early in November, Paul was in New Guinea. It is believed that Paul is Calhoun County's second service man to be killed in action in this war, it being reported this week also that Merle Holm of Lake City was killed in action on November 26. No details of the engagement, which took Paul's life, were received.

The telegram wire was sent 11:09 a.m. Dec. 24:

Mr. William Cavanaugh
Lohrville, Iowa

The Secretary of War desires me to express his deep
regret that your son, Private Paul J. Cavanaugh was
killed in action in defense of his country in the
southwest Pacific area. December 5th. Letter follows.

Ulio, the Adjutant General

Killed In Action

Word was received Monda...
om the War Department tha'
'ivate Merle Holm, 22, above
n of Andy Holm of Lake City,
s killed in action in the South
eific November 26, 1942. He

Merle Holm, one of the four men that
went with Paul to Fort Des Moines on
12/31/41. Companies K & I (Merle's &
Paul's respectively) were assigned the
Roadblock.

The Holm family of Lake City
would have received a similar
telegram announcing the death of
their son, Merle. Merle's mother
passed one year earlier.

Bill and Greta were not
notified of the telegram until
January 29, 1943, after school had
resumed. Father Kolvek, of Saint
Joseph's, asked Grandpa to come
into town and at that time told him
the news. The priest told Grandpa
he was too tender-hearted to tell
Grandma and suggested Grandpa
take Mom, who at the time was
teaching fifth grade at the Lohrville
Community school.

Mom and Grandpa broke
Grandma the news. Mom
remembers Grandma saying she
suspected something was wrong
when the priest had called and
asked Grandpa to meet him at
Saint Joseph's in Lohrville.

According to Melody, Paul was promoted to corporal in the field. Paul's gravestone says Cpl. but no paper work indicates that to be the case. If Paul were promoted (and probably was), the VOCO came up to him and said, "You're a corporal now." VOCO stood for, "Vocal Order Commanding Officer," the captain of your company, in Paul's case, John Shirley or possibly Meredith Huggins. Some of the men I interviewed said that, if offered, they would have refused a field commission because it would be a suicide wish, snipers were constantly gunning for officers.

During the rest of December, the Sanananda offensive fell into three main categories: attempts to break through the Roadblock, attempts to get supplies to the Roadblock, and Japanese attacks on the Roadblock. Surrounded and desperately fighting to defend the Roadblock throughout December, the soldiers prevailed and ultimately the "Buna" campaign was declared a victory on January 22, 1943 when the final and longest battle of the three-pronged campaign concluded with the defeat of the Japanese stronghold in Sanananda.

Grandpa and Grandma struggled with the news of Paul's death. When the war was over they bought the Clark farm. It was too difficult to stay on the home place. Dad returned from the war, and he and Mom moved onto the home place to farm. Greta's sister, who had one child, Cecil, commented to Grandma that since she had seven other children she should try to console herself at the loss of her one son. She had other children to be grateful for. Grandma told me that her sister didn't understand that no matter how many kids you had, the loss of one child among many is no less painful than the loss of an only child.

The Americans erected a memorial in the clearing that became known as the Huggin's Roadblock. I believe Paul is buried on the eastern half of the oval perimeter dissected by the Sanananda Road, 4½ miles north of Soputa.

The Japanese also erected a memorial stone to their Japanese fallen soldiers. The stone is inscribed with these words, "The war dead from Kochi-ken lies here. 1974, July; Governor of Kochi, Kochi-ken, Masumi Mizobuchi, representative of bereaved New Guinea society." Kochi City is near the mouth of Niyodo River on the Island of Shikoku and the home of the men Paul fought.

Kochi City is near the mouth of Niyodo River on the Island of Shikoku and the home of the men Paul fought. The Niyodo River is known in Japan as having the clearest water of any river in the country.

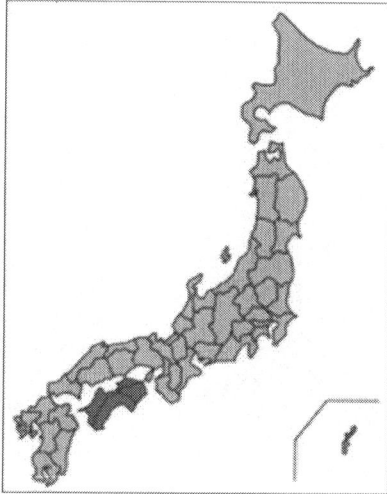

Shikoku, Japan

Japanese memorial on the Roadblock to this day.

Sanananda Village on the northern shoreline of New Guinea.

Chapter 10

Fallen Soldier

When a soldier fell, one dog tag was left with his body and one was given to the company commander, in Paul's case, Meredith Huggins, John Shirley's replacement. Huggins was wounded the 5th and returned to the Roadblock on the 8th. Fallen soldiers inside the Roadblock were buried where they fell as quickly as possible. Merle Holm was killed when Company I and K entered the swamps on November 26 to flank the Japanese in an effort to secure the Roadblock. His body was never recovered and was probably lost in the jungle swamp near the Roadblock.

Sometimes there was barely enough dirt to bury soldiers. Van Hammen shared that he still has nightmares of burying soldiers in ground that contained more water than dirt. He can still smell the stench, hear girgles, and see the bubbles coming up from shallow, water-laden graves. A few bodies were carried back of the lines for temporary burial, later to be uncovered and transported to a permanent cemetery. The vets I interviewed knew that efforts were made by the Graves Administration to locate the men temporarily buried on the Roadblock during the battle. They also thought that since the government declared Paul's remains unrecoverable, his body had been overlooked in search attempts, something easy to do with all the jungle foliage. Paul apparently, as his record indicates, is buried on the east side of the Sanananda Track, 4 ½ miles north of Soputa, search area #78-A to this day. Mass graves were also dug. Melody helped with that, as did some of the natives. Australians, Japanese, and Americans were all raked into a common grave. Van Hammen said he smelled like a dead person after burying so many soldiers.

When Melody returned from New Guinea, Grandpa and

Grandma told them they wanted Paul's remains brought home. Melody discouraged them from that explaining that since the water table was so high and the jungle so hot, bodies decomposed quickly and they would only receive a box full of New Guinea mud.

Melody was shot in the stomach in the Buna campaign but recovered. On his first night back, several months later, he was ordered to patrol the same trail he was wounded on some months earlier. Upon returning to Australia, Melody wrote a letter to his brother that was published in the hometown newspaper:

New Guinea Vet Writes Brother
Cpl. Raymond Melody in Buna Campaign
2/10/43

Dear Tom,

I know it has been some time since I have written to you, but as you perhaps have noted I have been very busy the last few months, but I am OK now and I am back in good old Australia in a rest area, and don't think it don't seem good to get back where there is a little night life again.

I hope I never see New Guinea again, rec'd 42 letters the first day I got back from the front and many more since, and your Christmas box was swell, everything I could use.

How is Pat and the boys, I would sure like to see them, but don't suppose I will have much chance for some time, but this war may not last too long as those damn Japs are not so tuff as everyone thought they were, and I spent 41 days and nights finding that out.

I was made a corporal the other day. I guess this army is getting short of men or something. Have you heard from Don lately and where is he now? I hope still in the good old U.S.A., and I am glad he is with the air force as that is a good branch of the service.

It was too bad about Paul Cavanaugh, he was a swell guy and a good soldier, his folks should be very proud of him.

Well Tom, I can't think of any other news, so write soon.

Your brother,
Cpl. Ray (Ha)

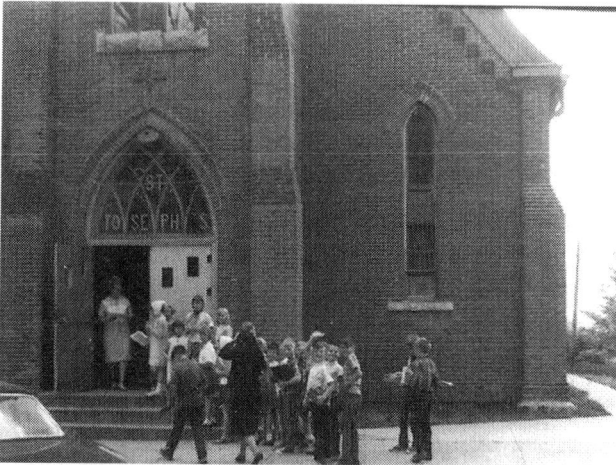

Saint Joseph's Catholic Church where Grandpa was told of Paul's death.

Chapter 11

In Memory

On March 28, 1943, "somewhere in the South Pacific," a memorial service was held in honor of the 126th who laid down their lives in New Guinea. Joseph Sladen Bradley, the commanding officer of the 126th Infantry Regiment unit, at that time, gave the address:

> We pause today to do honor to the members of this gallant regiment who have paid, the supreme sacrifice in laying down their lives in the performance of their duty on the field of battle in New Guinea.
>
> Their names are indelibly inscribed upon the Roll of Honor of our country. They have willingly laid down their lives for freedom, for their families, and for their homes. Their contribution to our effort, their deeds, and acts of gallantry have played a vital part in the victory achieved in our baptism of fire, and during our mortal engagement with a fierce and determined enemy. We shall cherish their memory, and in this, our current training period, the inspiration they have given us will help us to steel our nerves and to skill ourselves so that we may avenge their sacrifices.
>
> We stand bareheaded to salute them, to reaffirm our allegiance, our devotion, our faith, and to express our determined will to destroy this enemy, and to demonstrate to our departed comrades and their loved ones that we shall endeavor to our uttermost to keep unsullied and untarnished the enviable record of heroism they have established ...

Melody was incorrectly listed as KIA under Company C in the memorial record. Paul and Merle Holm were listed as KIA from Company I and Company K, respectively. George Frotscher's name doesn't appear, and as confirmed later, returned home to farm on the opposite side of the section that Earl Davis of Lohrville was born and raised on. Davis knew Frotscher well. He said Frotscher always asked him how his crops were doing and regardless of how good Davis's crops were, Frotscher always said his were better.

Paul was awarded the Bronze Star, Philippine Presidential Unit Citation, Purple Heart, Good Conduct Medal, Asiatic-Pacific Campaign Medal, WWII Victory Medal, the Presidential Unit emblem, and the honorable service lapel button. There is a plaque for Paul in the Manila cemetery. His highest honor was the Bronze Star.

Paul purchased a life insurance policy when he entered the military worth $1,200 that was used to purchase a home for his Grandma Leonard in Lohrville. I have been told the policy was in Marilyn's name.

Grandpa and Grandma began a correspondence with the government to secure Uncle Paul's remains. Years passed before Grandpa and Grandma received word from the government that Paul's remains were not among the "unknowns" (based on unmatched dental records) or "knowns" and was, therefore, conclusively considered unrecoverable. Though Paul's body was deemed unrecoverable in 1950, his body must have been found since his personal effects were returned home. They were shipped in one package weighing one pound. Inside the box was Paul's rosary with a note: "Send to William Cavanaugh." Also included in his personal effects were several pictures and his birth record indicating Grandpa's and Grandma's names and address.

Paul's body may have been lost in a temporary grave or in one of the mass graves Van Hammen was assigned to. According to Van Hammen, many Americans and Japanese were buried temporarily and some in mass graves after the conflict.

THE UNITED STATES OF AMERICA

TO ALL WHO SHALL SEE THESE PRESENTS, GREETING: THIS IS TO CERTIFY THAT THE PRESIDENT
OF THE UNITED STATES OF AMERICA AUTHORIZED BY EXECUTIVE ORDER, 24 AUGUST 1962 HAS AWARDED

THE BRONZE STAR MEDAL

TO

PRIVATE PAUL J. CAVANAUGH, UNITED STATES ARMY

FOR

meritorious achievement in ground combat against the armed enemy
during World War II in the Asiatic Pacific Theater of Operations.

GIVEN UNDER MY HAND IN THE CITY OF WASHINGTON
THIS 21st DAY OF May 19 90

Paul's Bronze Star

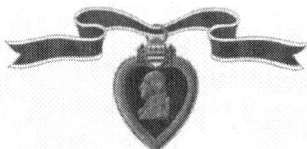

THE UNITED STATES OF AMERICA

TO ALL WHO SHALL SEE THESE PRESENTS, GREETING:

THIS IS TO CERTIFY THAT
THE PRESIDENT OF THE UNITED STATES OF AMERICA
HAS AWARDED THE

PURPLE HEART

ESTABLISHED BY GENERAL GEORGE WASHINGTON
AT NEWBURGH, NEW YORK, AUGUST 7, 1782
TO

PRIVATE PAUL J. CAVANAUGH, UNITED STATES ARMY

FOR WOUNDS RECEIVED
IN ACTION
ASIATIC PACIFIC THEATER OF OPERATIONS 5 DECEMBER 1942
GIVEN UNDER MY HAND IN THE CITY OF WASHINGTON
THIS 21st DAY OF May 19 90

Paul's Purple Heart

After the war, Bill and Greta bought the James Clark place. Staying in the home place was too difficult with all the memories of Paul. Bernice remembers visiting Grant Wood, the artist, who would rent a room from the Clarks for rural inspiration.

Rosary, baptismal record, personal photos found on Paul's body.

The military sent Grandpa and Grandma a letter asking if Paul was married or had a will in order to determine who to send his effects back to. In response to their letter, Grandma wrote this note,

> Lohrville, Ia; June 19, 1943
> L. E. Millinckrodt, 2nd Lt. d.m.g. Asst. Effects d. m.
>
> Dear Sir:
>
> Your letter came. We are indeed deeply grieved over the loss of our Darling son. His death has made us very bitter and the tragic part *is that* he *is* so far from home. He wasn't given a fair deal. Scarcely 13 weeks on this side then shipped across. He never had a furlough.
>
> His personal items will be appreciated – We would like his body returned to us. Neither have we received his back pay. Thank you so much for your deep sympathy,
>
> Sincerely,
> Mr. and Mrs. W. P. Cavanaugh

14135   Lohrville, Ia.
                              June 19, 1943

L. E. Millinebrost
2nd Lt.   Q.M.C.   asst. Effects Q.M.

Dear Sir:
        Your letter came. We are indeed deeply grieved over the loss of our Darling son.
        His death has made us very bitter & the tragic part he so far from home.
        He wasn't given a fair deal, scarcely 18 weeks on this side then shipped across. He never had a furlough.
        His home was in our home, he was not married neither did he have a will.
        His personal items will be appreciated.
        We would like his body returned to us.
        Neither have we received his back pay.
        Thank you so much for your deep sympathy. Sincerely —
                Mr & Mrs W. P. Cavanaugh

Written Request

WAR DEPARTMENT
ARMY EFFECTS BUREAU

ORDER FOR SHIPMENT

Case No. 14135 D
Date June 30, 1943

MEMORANDUM to Warehouse -
Please see that the personal effects on the above mentioned case are packed, weighed and ready for shipment promptly so that they may be readily picked up. Bills of Lading and all other papers will be marked with the case number and can be identified thereby. The original of this form should be returned to the office after completion.

Effects of: Pvt. Paul J. Cavanaugh   Serial No: 37,111,184

Ship to: Mr. William Cavanaugh

Address: Lohrville, Iowa

Ship Via: Franked   Gov't B/L No.

For the Effects Quartermaster

LIST OF PACKAGES SHIPPED

1 Pkg.

Franked Mail (4 lbs or less) **
Parcel Post Charges -
Estimated Express Charges -
Estimated Freight Charges -

Total Number of Pieces: 1   Checked by: J.MINOTTI, 1st Lt. Q.M.C.
Weight of Shipment: 12   Date: 7/1/43

Effects QM Form No. 14 (Revised 1-7-43)

WAR DEPARTMENT

611 Hardesty Avenue

July 5, 1945

Mr. and Mrs. E. F. Cavanaugh
Lohrville
Iowa

Dear Mr. and Mrs. Cavanaugh:

Thank you for your letter of June 19th furnishing us the information we requested in connection with the disposition of a few items of personal property which belonged to your son, Private Paul J. Cavanaugh. These items have been forwarded to you by mail, under separate cover.

Attached is a receipt form covering the property sent to you. This should be signed by Mr. Cavanaugh and may be witnessed by Mrs. Cavanaugh or a friend. So that our records may be complete, I will appreciate your returning one copy of the signed receipt to me.

My action in forwarding these effects does not, of itself, vest legal title to them in you. I transmit these items only in order that some responsible individual receive them who is willing and able to properly distribute the same in accordance with the laws of the state in which your son lived.

With reference to your claims relative to back pay, the pay records of soldiers are in the custody of the General Accounting Office, Washington, D.C. and it is suggested that you write to that office regarding any allowance due.

It is my understanding that no arrangements have been made for the return of remains to the United States until after the cessation of hostilities. This Bureau does not itself handle such matters, consequently any additional inquiries you may have concerning the return of your son's body should be addressed to the Memorial Division, Office of The Quartermaster General, Washington 25, D.C.

I sincerely regret that the personal belongings of your son were not recovered, and wish to assure you that in the event any additional property of Private Cavanaugh is forwarded to us, you will be notified immediately.

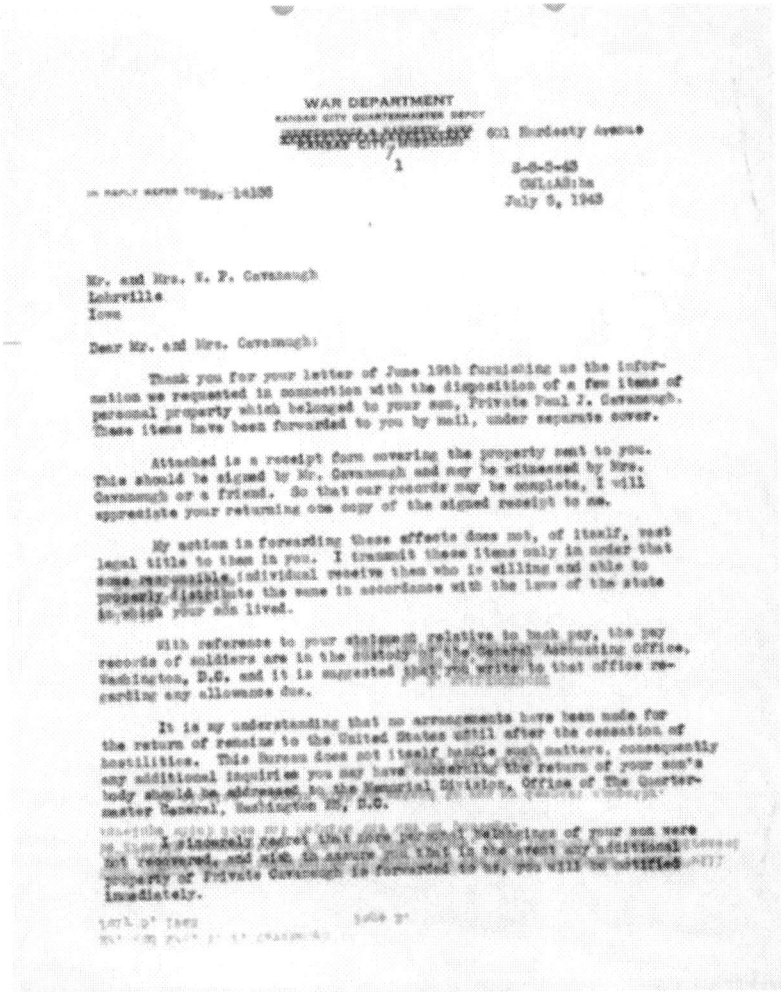

As requested, Grandpa and Grandma returned the form indicating they had received Paul's personal items in the self-addressed, stamped envelope provided by the government.

1 Rosary, 1 birth record, and several pictures were found on Paul's body before buried in the field.

July 12, 1943
Lohrville, Iowa

Memorial Division
Office of the Quartermaster
Washington, DC

I'm writing you in regards of the remains of our loving son. Who was killed in the Buna battle, New Guinea? We would like to have some information on this matter. We want his remains returned to us.

Very Truly Yours,
Mrs. W P. Cavanaugh

Written Request

21 July 1943
Address Reply to the Quartermaster General
Mrs. W. P. Cavanaugh,
Lohrville, Iowa

Dear Mrs. Cavanaugh:

Acknowledgment is made of your letter of recent
date, regarding the return of the remains of your son,
the late Pvt. Paul J. Cavanaugh to...

It is regretted to have to advise you that for military
reasons, it became necessary to adopt the policy that
the remains of military personnel who die at stations
outside the continental limits of the United States
shall be interred locally until after cessation of
hostilities when sympathetic consideration will be
given the question of their return for final internment.
The graves of our service men are so marked and
recorded as to preserve their identity as far as
humanly possible until removal to this country can be
permitted.

Please be advised that a notation has been made on
the official records of this office that it is your desire
to have the remains of your son returned, if possible,
to the United States for final interment, and at the
proper time you will be contacted in order to obtain
the latest shipping instructions and action will be
taken at that time to carry out your request and the
remains will be prepared and shipped at Government
expense to the place thus designated by you.

I feel deep sorrow for you and your family in your bereavement and may you come to bear it bravely and proudly because of the courage and ideals that his life and service for his country exemplified.

For the Quartermaster General.

Very truly yours,
R. P. Harbold, Colonel, QMC, Assistant
Unknown Date

Lohrville, Iowa
Lt C. R. Gash:

Dear Sir:

Listed in today's paper are the names of 110 Iowan's bodies on US Army Transport Lt. George W. G. Boyce docking in the near future at San Francisco, California among the dead are the names of some of the boys from New Guinea who fought and died with "Our Paul." (Pvt Paul J. Cavanaugh 37111184)) What's wrong? Didn't we take the proper procedure to have our son's remains returned to his homeland after his death in '42. I wrote in to Washington and advised the I. M. Department we wanted his body sent home. In a reply letter, they promised it would be returned. Boys who were killed months afterward are returned home.

Sincerely Yours,
Mrs. W. P Cavanaugh
Lohrville, Iowa

Johnville ___

Lt. Co. R. Yest:

Dear Sir:

Listed in todays paper are the names of 110 Iowans bodies on U.S. army transport Lt George W. G. Boyce docking in the near future at ___ Francisco Cal. among the dead are the names of some of the boys from New Hamer who fought & died with "Our Paul". (Pvt Paul J. Cavanaugh 37111184)

Whats wrong? Didnt we take the proper procedure to have our sons remains returned to his home land. After his death in '42 I wrote into Washington & advised the Q.M. Depot we wanted his body sent home. In a reply letter they promised it would be Returned. Boys who were Killed months afterward are returned home.

Sincerely yours.

Mrs W. P. Cavanaugh.
Johnville Ia.

Written Request

23 February 1944

SPQYH 293
Cavanaugh Paul J.
Mr. W. P. Cavanaugh,
Lohrville, Iowa

Dear Mr. Cavanaugh:

Reference is made to your application for a
Government flat marble marker for the grave of the
late Paul J. Cavanaugh, who was killed in action, and
which you desire to be furnished as a memorial to
him.

It is deeply regretted that you must be advised that
this office has no authority to furnish a headstone
under such circumstances, as these stones are
furnished for the unmarked graves of deceased
members of the Armed Forces of the United States.
If the remains of this veteran are returned to the
United States, after the cessation of hostilities, a
Government marker will be furnished upon request.

This office understands your feelings to have a
marker in memory of the decedent, and it is sincerely
regretted that it has been necessary to advise that one
cannot be furnished.

For the Quartermaster General:

Very truly yours,
R. P. Harbold, Colonel, Q. M. Corps, Assistant

27 December 1945

Address Reply to
The Quartermaster General
Attention: Memorial Division

Mr. William Cavanaugh
Lohrville, Iowa
Dear Mr. Cavanaugh:

The War Department is now taking steps to furnish regulation burial flags in memory of military personnel whose remains have not been recovered or were buried at sea.

I regret to inform you that there is nothing in the official records of this office to indicate that the remains of your son, the late Private Paul J. Cavanaugh, were recovered. Therefore, an application for a flag is enclosed with an envelope, which requires no postage for its return to this office. Upon receipt of the application signed by you, steps will be taken to furnish a regulation flag in his memory.

May our country's flag be an everlasting symbol that these heroic men did not die in vain.

For the Quartermaster General:

Sincerely yours,
James L Prenn
Major, QMC
Assistant

6 January 1947

In Reply Refer to
QMGMR 293
Cavanaugh, Paul J.
SN 37 111 184

SUBJECT: Additional Information That May Lead to the Recovery and Identification of Remains Not Yet Accounted For

TO: Commanding Officer
American Graves Registration Service Area Command
Pacific Theater
APO 707, c/o Postmaster
San Francisco, California

1. Reference it made to letter this office, QMGYG 314.6, Subject: Addition Methods of Locating and Identifying unknowns and Resolving Cases of Remains Not Yet Recovered, dated 4 October 1946.

2. Attached hereto, in duplicate, is OQMG Form 371 for the following deceased individual whose remains have not yet been recovered or identified: Cavanaugh, Paul J. Private 37 111 184

3. It is requested that every attempt be made by your command to locate or identify remains of this individual and the results of your investigation, whether positive or negative, be returned to this office by endorsement hereon, within 60 days of receipt of this communication.

For the Quartermaster General:
Martin G. Riley
Major, QMCX, Assistant

8 May 1947

SUBJECT: Identification of Unknown Deceased

TO: Commanding General, Philippine-Ryukyus Command, APO 707, c/o Postmaster, San Francisco, California

Reference is made to 2nd Ind Dated 13 Jan 47 your headquarters, File QSQMM, Subj: Comparison of Dental Charts. The dental records of the following individuals will be compared with the records of the Unknown X-Numbers indicated interred in Finschhafen #2, N. G.:

Name		X-Number
Cavanaugh, Paul J.	37111184	X-33, 35, 37, 172
Borders, Andrew J.	0-728558	
Buchannon, Jess C.	36112411	
Barron, John M.	36321185	

For the Quartermaster General:
James C. MacFarland
Major, QMC
Memorial Division

April 16, 1948
Quarter Master

Dear Sirs:

I hardly know what to say or where to begin. I wanted to inquire about our son's body: Pvt. Paul J. Cavanaugh 37111184 Lohrville, Iowa. He was killed in New Guinea, Dec 5, 1942. When will his remains be returned to us & why didn't it come from Australia on the other large shipment of bodies? Waiting a reply.

Sincerely,
Mr. and Mrs. W.P. Cavanaugh
Lake City, Iowa

Written Request

20 April 1948

Mr. & Mrs. W. P. Cavanaugh
Lake City, Iowa

Dear Mr. And Mrs. Cavanaugh:

This refers to your letter concerning the return of
your late son's remains to this country for final burial.

In view of your statement that your son was killed in
New Guinea, we assume that he may have been
buried in one of the Finschhafen Cemeteries.
Information available here indicates that those
remains originally interred in the Finschhafen
Cemeteries have been temporarily concentrated into
the Luzon Mausoleum in order to facilitate
repatriation activities. Under the present program,
which is subject to revision, returns from Luzon are
scheduled at reasonable intervals during, and possibly
beyond, the period from the present through October
1948.

With reference to your inquiry as to why your son's
remains were not in the shipment returned from
Australia. The port of call for New Guinea remains
will be Manila, Luzon, unless present plans are
changed. Please be assured that this office will contact
the legal next of kin when we are notified that the
remains are en route to the United States port.

If further questions arise and you reel that we can be
of assistance to you, please call on us.

Sincerely, yours,

Cr. Yost
Lt. Colonel, mc
Chief, American Graves Registration Div.

7 June 1948

Mrs. W. P. Cavanaugh
Lohrville, Iowa
Dear Mrs. Cavanaugh:

I refer to our correspondence regarding your late son,
Private Paul J. Cavanaugh.

Since no information concerning your late son has
been received here as yet, I have forwarded your
letter to the Quartermaster General, Memorial
Division, Washington 25, D. C., for reply direct to
you. Please be assured that you will hear from
Washington within a reasonable amount of time.

If I may be of further assistance to you, please feel
free to call on me.

Sincerely yours,

Frederick E. Hyll
Major, QMC
Assistant Chief
American Graves Registration Div.

28 June 1948

Mrs. W.P. Cavanaugh
Lake City, Iowa
Dear Mrs. Cavanaugh:

Your letter to the chief, American graves registration division, Kansas City Quartermaster Depot, Kansas City, Missouri, concerning your son, the late Private Paul J. Cavanaugh, has been referred to this office.

With deep regret, I must inform you that no information has been received in this office indicating that the remains of your son have been recovered.

A continuous and intensive search is being made of the area in which he died, and it is my sincere hope that it will be possible to recover and rebury the remains of your son in an established military cemetery.

Although fully understanding your natural anxiety I regret that I cannot assure you that it will be possible to return the remains of your son until a report of burial is received.

Every effort is being made to recover and positively identify all remains of our heroic dead. Meanwhile, please rest assured that when a report is received I shall immediately notify you,

Sincerely, yours,

Richard B. Coombs Major, QMC
Memorial Division

On September 9, 1949, O. E. Van Horn, the Adjutant American Legion Post 368 of Lohrville, Iowa submitted Grandma's application to the Executive Secretary of the Service Compensation Board in Des Moines with supporting documents of compensation recovery.

16 March 1950

CASE HISTORY FOR REMAINS CONSIDERED NON-RECOVERABLE

Cavanaugh, Paul J.
Pvt 37 111 184

BASIS FOR DECLARING REMAINS NON-RECOVERABLE

1. Attached OQMG Form 371 reveals that Pvt. Paul J. Cavanaugh, 37 111 184, was "killed in action" in the Soputa area of Southeastern Australian New Guinea Island, on 5 Dec. 1942. However, subject decedent was not a recorded known burial in any cemetery under the jurisdiction of this Hqs.

2. Further investigation of this case reveals the following information:

    a. The final area search and recovery operations conducted by American Graves Registration Service search and Recovery teams in the Southeastern Australian New Guinea area have been completed. Administration check of records in this office, however, fails to reveal the remains of Pvt. Cavanaugh as having been recovered as a "known" from this area.

    b. Identification data for all applicable "unknowns" recovered from the Southeastern Australian New Guinea area (Philcom Zone Search Area #78) have been compared with the identifying data shown on the attached OQMG Form 371 for Pvt. Cavanaugh in an effort to associate same with subject decedent, but results were negative.

3. Findings and recommendations are based on all available information.

4. It is recommended that the remains of Pvt. Paul J. Cavanaugh, 37 111 184, be considered non-recoverable and all records pertaining thereto be closed.

Approval Recommended: Charles R. Whaylen; William B Jackson; Harold B McNemar

16 May 1950

QMCMF 293
Cavanaugh, Paul
SN 37111184

Mrs. And Mrs. William Cavanaugh

Lohrville, Iowa
Dear Mr. And Mrs. Cavanaugh:

Several years have lapsed since the cessation of hostilities of World War II, which cost the life of your son, the late Private Paul J. Cavanaugh.

It is with deep regret that your Government finds it necessary to inform you that further search and investigation have failed to reveal the whereabouts of your son's remains. Since all efforts to recover and identify his remains have failed, it has been necessary to declare that his remains are not recoverable.

Realizing the extent of your great loss, it is with reluctance that you are sent the information that there is no grave at which to pay homage. May the knowledge of your son's honorable service to his country be a source of sustaining comfort to you.

Sincerely yours,

J. F. Vogl
Captain, QMC
Memorial Division

My June 15, 1989 request for Paul's burial records.

On Sunday, January 26, 2014, I received a surprising phone call from Sharon Elliott a professional genealogist working for the United States Army. She was looking for relatives of a particular soldier killed in WWII, Paul Cavanaugh. She explained to me that some remains had been located and it was possible that Uncle Paul's remains could be among them. She was part of the "No Soldier Left Behind" program being carried out by the Army Past Conflict Repatriation

Branch of the Army. The National Guard comes under their umbrella. She emphasized there was no guarantee that Paul's remains would be among the ones found and now in a lab in Hawai'i.

Mrs. Elliott first contacted Marcella Judson as Paul's sister and living next of kin in an attempt to acquire the DNA from Paul's "female side" which carries the mitochondria. Mrs. Elliott spoke with Steve Judson, Marcella's son. Steve gave them my number as the "male side" carrying Paul's "Y" DNA, both helpful in matching DNA samples from the remains. Mrs. Elliott was interested in my sending her a copy of *Somewhere in the South Pacific.* She also gave me a web page the Army set up for families to track the efforts of this search, www.dpmo.com, and the phone number for the Army Casualty Center.

In calling the Army Casualty Center, I learned more. I spoke with Cherri Lawless of Fort Knox who works as a liaison between different agencies associated with recovery efforts. One of these agencies is the Joint Prisoners of War Missing in Action Accounting Command (JPAC) who heads up recovery efforts. I explained to Ms. Lawless the location of Paul's body: 4½ miles north of Saputa on the Saputa/Sanananda trail and on the east side of the trail in what was the Huggin's Roadblock. I asked her if that is where these remains were coming from. She said, "yes." I was dumbfounded, that's an area not much bigger than a football field. She said that over the years, new technology has developed and sometimes individual siting reports cause the JPAC to investigate possible leads. Again, there was no guarantee, but there is definitely the possibility that Paul's remains could be among those recently found.

Mrs. Elliott said salt water can help preserve remains, even though New Guinea's climate might facilitate decay. I was told to expect the DNA swab kit within one-two weeks and once received, my DNA would be compared to the DNA samples of the remains now in a lab in Hawai'i.. My DNA would stay on the record for any possible finds in the future. Cherri Lawless also requested a copy of this book, *Somewhere in the South Pacific.* After receiving my DNA sample, I was told it would take 9-24 months for a match to be confirmed. If there is a positive match, the next of kin, Marcella Judson, would be given the remains and the authority to decide where they are buried. If Marcella is unable to serve as Paul's next of kin, the oldest of Paul's sibling's children, John William Cavanaugh, will become the next of kin. We will not be notified if there is no match.

Ms. Lawless sent me an electronic file of Paul's records, some, of which, I had never seen. I was surprised to find in Paul's file from the Army Past Conflict Repatriation Branch a letter I wrote nearly 30 years ago seeking Uncle Paul's burial records.

On January 30, 2014, I received the DNA swath kit. I filled out the paperwork and drove to Mom's for her to sign as a witness that I swabbed three samples from the inside of my cheek. Mom cut Paul's hair the night before he left and now was serving to help identify his body 72 years later. The samples were sent in the mail that day and now, the clock is ticking on the 9-24 months response as to whether Paul's remains have been found.

My son, Ryan, and I attended a "No Soldier's Left Behind" meeting in Denver and enjoyed meeting many who lost loved ones in War or have loved ones missing in action. The US government uses these events to give updates on efforts to locate bodies. After attending this meeting, I realized it would be nearly miraculous for Paul's remains to be recovered. Not long after this, however, my sister sent a newspaper article sharing the story of one GI whose remains from New Guinea were identified.

Chapter 12

Conclusion

I woke to the sound of a shotgun blast on Memorial Day, 1972. Half awake, half asleep, my mind tried to fabricate a reason for the sound I just heard. I wandered from one scenario to the next. Was someone hunting? That didn't make sense. Did the gas tank at the hog house explode? Maybe, but unlikely. Suddenly I was fully awake as I heard my sister, Sue, yell, "Tim, Dad's been hurt." I jumped out of bed and bolted downstairs. Dad's arms had been severely burned. I hopped into a truck with our hired man, Carl Johnson, and together we drove down the road to what was Grandpa and Grandma's home, now a cumulous, dark, black, rumbling cloud of smoke racing into the sky. When we pulled up to the home, the west wall had been blown off the house into the lane. The other three walls were still connected to one another but askew to the foundation. The roof was resting

Home of William and Greta Cavanaugh days after a furnace explosion destroyed it on Memorial Day, 1972.

askew on the walls. The house burned to the ground within minutes as dazed survivors made their way out of the rubble and into the lane for help. I found out later that two cousins sleeping upstairs had literally been blown out the roof of the house into the backyard on their mattresses! Grandpa approached our vehicle repeatedly saying, "My beautiful house." Most of the family would spend weeks and even months at the local hospital recovering from these burns, but fortunately, no one was killed. Only two family photographs blown out and away from the house as it burned down, survived this calamity, both were photos of Paul Cavanaugh as an infant.

Pulitzer Prize winning writer, Clark Mollenhoff[30], lived in Lohrville and is buried at the St. Joseph's Catholic cemetery. His poem *Old Bill,* is about Paul's father, William Cavanaugh, but references Paul. Grandpa's sentiment at the end of this poem can easily be the sentiment we all share as we read Paul's story and reflect on our own travels through this world with it's many "heartaches and ecstatic joys," "poverties and plenties," "good times and tears."

Old Bill

"We were a team," he said to let us know
That life with Greta gone was not the same.
"I'm ready now. I think it's time to go."
His bright expressive eyes disguised his age.
His eager talk of politics was clear,
And yet Old Bill had reached the stage
When death's approach produced no trace of fear.

In ninety years, Old Bill had seen it all,
From heartbreak to the most ecstatic joys.
A far-off war had cut down handsome Paul.
God spared the other seven, girls and boys.

Bill spoke each name with special father's pride,
And smiled deep satisfaction with his life.
Life had been good, though one of eight had died,
For he had shared it with a loving wife.

Through poverty and plenty they had worked,
From youthful romance through the trying years.
An optimistic Greta never shirked –
Was energetic through good times and tears.

Bill's eyes welled up again at Greta's name.
"We were a team," he said. His voice was low.
"With Greta gone the pleasure's not the same.
"I'm ready now. I think it's time to go."

What do we take away from Paul Cavanaugh's life story? One vet I interviewed said he walked away from Buna with "eternal friendship." I'm sure the camaraderie of war rivets men together as nothing else can and, indeed, there is good that can come of these horrible events.

Nonetheless, as I walk away from this study looking for the redeeming value of it all, I am left feeling very sad and am left with a sense of great loss this war brought upon a loving, vital, hope-filled individual, Paul Cavanaugh, and his family – my family. I know that though writing this book helped me better understand that loss, it's those who knew Paul personally who understand the darkness of that loss most.

I walk away sobered by the debased nature of mankind and how that nature can stoop to such great depths of evil. I'm left recognizing that great evil requires great courage, endurance, suffering, and not too infrequently, the loss of life.

I hope this paper honors the memory of my uncle who engaged in the front-line combat against the evil of his day. Today's evils require the same courage and tenacity of spirit and perhaps, in order to be defeated, even the loss of loved ones just as it was required "somewhere in the South Pacific" in Paul's day.

Given the reality of evil in this world, for me and simply put, I can't have my "Iowa" without my "Buna," and I can't have my "Buna" without my faith that there is a good God who rewards those who seek Him (Hebrews 11:6).

Grand Rapid's own, Kimberly Gill's, *Fading Warriors*, honors the memory of those men from the 32ⁿᵈ Red Arrow Division that fought in New Guinea and have and are coming to the end of their lives. I interviewed Bob Van Hammen (Company I; center, left), now deceased during my research. The other two men are local to Grand Rapids. One of them is Kimberly Gill's father, Jack Hill; the third, Russell Prince. Images from *Nightmare in New Guinea* are embedded in the painting.

Appendix

The Photo

Dyersville, Iowa boasts of being the birth place of George Strock whose WWII photograph of dead Americans on a Buna Beach has been called "The photo that won World War II." Up until its publication on September 20, 1943, the United States government prohibited any photograph be published depicting dead American soldiers. Thanks to a 25-year-old correspondent named Cal Whipple, Strock's was the first photo published depicting dead American soldiers on Buna Beach on December 31, 1942. These three men died on the beach which came to be known as Maggot Beach in the same battle that Uncle Paul was killed in twenty-five days earlier and miles away.

Whipple was assigned the Pentagon for *LIFE* magazine. There he waged a war of his own but with the United States government's censor department who feared such photographs would demoralize the American public. Whipple went from captain to major to colonel to general to the assistant secretary of the Air Corps and then to the White House for permission to publish Strock's photo. He argued that though the War was far from over and the outcome far from certain, many Americans seemed to be growing complacent over the War. He believed Strock's photograph would stir the American conscience to fight on. Finally, the authorities consented. The military only insisted that their faces not be shown or the insignia of the units they belonged to. These three men remain anonymous today. *LIFE* published the photograph with this statement:

> Here lie three Americans. What shall we say of them? Shall we say that this is a noble sight? Shall we

say that this is a fine thing, that they should give their lives for their country? Or shall we say that this is too horrible to look at? Why print this picture, anyway, of three American boys dead upon an alien shore? Is it to hurt people? To be morbid? Those are not the reasons. The reason is that words are never enough. The eye sees. The mind knows. The heart feels. But the words do not exist to make us see, or know, or feel what it is like, what actually happens. The words are never right. The reason we print it now is that, last week, President Roosevelt and Elmer Davis (Director of the Office of War Information), and the War Department decided that the American people ought to be able to see their own boys as they fall in battle; to come directly and without words into the presence of their own dead. And so here it is. This is the reality that lies behind the names that come to rest at last on monuments in the leafy squares of busy American towns.

Strock gave added insight to the challenge of the Buna campaign in a letter he wrote from Buna on December 17, 1942:

Must admit that it's tough work as well as being somewhat dangerous, but I have the feeling that nothing will happen to me, and so far, I'm right. Our clothes were wet for a week, it rains almost every night. Shoes have been soaked and there is very little chance to take them off because of a possibility of a night raid. We sleep in a helmet; this way we keep the head dry.

Strock once tried to take a bath but told his boss the groundwater smelled too much like dead bodies for him to do so.

Sources

Flyboys, James Bradley (author of *Flags of Our Fathers*)

The Ghost Mountain Boys, James Campbell

The American Legion, Sept. 1992

Lohrville Enterprise, "Paul Cavanaugh First Lohrville War Casualty" (January 28, 1943)

War in New Guinea, W. Martin King, 1944

Personal Diary, Edwin Wesholski, Company I (HQ)

Nightmare in New Guinea, Grand Valley State University History Department

Government Offices

    American Graves Registration Service

    Federal Records Center, Kansas City (for Paul's Military Records)

    National Archives

    Department of the Army, Army Awards

    The American Battle Monument Commission

    National Personnel Records Center

    Commission of Veteran Affairs, Rockwell City, IA 50579

    Iowa Department of Public Defense

    Iowa Department of Veteran Affairs

    General Service Administration

Grand Valley State University, Veteran's History Project

Steve Janicki, William Sikkel, Shirley Weber, (online videos)

Dr. James Smither (smitherj@gvsu.edu); 616-331-3422

Personal Interviews:

Raymond Melody (Company C), Lake City, IA (Pvt)

Meredith Huggins (Company I), Honolulu, HI (Captain)

Woodrow (Woody) Tromp (Company I), Grand Rapids, MI

Lawrence Edgington (Company I), Sac City, IA (Pvt)/Letter to Marcella

Earl Smested (Company I), Grand Rapids, MI (HQ, telephone)

Francis Homminga (Company I), Grand Rapids, MI (machine gunner)

Bob Van Hammen (Company I), Grand Rapids, MI

Esther Van Hammen (Bob's widow), Grand Rapids, MI

Family & Friends:

Bernice Chezlak, Gene Spenla, Leonard Cavanaugh, Marcella Judson, Esther Parker, Cecil Siemann, Earl Davis, Margaret Marie Fox, Clement Cavanaugh, Edythe Cavanaugh, Harry Kunkle, Joe Miller, William and Greta Cavanaugh

Endnotes

[1] A recent story was told of a woman in Papua New Guinea fighting desperately with a ten-foot crocodile as she tried in vain to save her daughter from its jaws. The girl was cleaning vegetables with her mother at the edge of a river when the saltwater crocodile lunged at her, clamping its mouth around her body. Helpless villagers watched as the mother grabbed her daughter's hand and attempted to pull her free from the predator's powerful jaws. The mother lost her grip and the crocodile dived beneath the water, dragging the girl down with it. Villagers reported that the crocodile disappeared into the waters then surfaced again with the girl still trapped in its jaws.

[2] Jungle Rot is a painful condition often initiated by minor trauma, usually below the knees of people with poor footwear and nutrition. Lesions begin with an inflammation that can progress into concentrated vesicles which, in turn, rupture into ulcers. Once developed, ulcers can become chronic and can continue into deep tissue creating a risk of amputation.

[3] Doctor Warmenhoven was from Hull, Iowa and served as one of the physicians for the 126th. Shortly after the Buna campaign was over and the troops were back in Australia, MacArthur pressured Warmenhoven to authorize the 126th's return to combat, which Warmenhoven refused to do. Doctor Warmenhoven committed suicide after returning to Australia from New Guinea and while recuperating at Camp Cable.

[4] The Rickettsia bacteria can cause various forms of Typhus (not to be confused with an entirely different disease, Typhoid fever). The bacteria can be transmitted by mites, rodents, fleas, or lice. The name comes from the Greek *"typhos"* meaning smoky or hazy, describing the state of mind of those afflicted.

[5] Athletes foot and jock rash are other common forms of fungal induced ringworm.

[6] General MacArthur replaced Harding (who he believed was not aggressive enough) with Eichelberger.

[7] The New Guinea campaign simply referred to as "Buna," was, in fact, a three-pronged Allied offensive against the Japanese based in Gona, Sanananda, and Buna. The Australians constituted one prong against the Japanese in Gona, Paul's 126th was the second prong against the Japanese at Sanananda, and the 2nd Battalion, under Major Smith, was the third prong against the Japanese in Buna. Smith's group was called the Ghost Mountain Boys. They deployed from Port Moresby to a Kapa Kapa staging area on the southern coastline of New Guinea. They marched north on the Kapa Kapa trail to Jaure and then joined the 128th in an assault against Buna, though originally scheduled to join the 126th against Sanananda. Ghost Mountain is a peak in the Kapa Kapa trail known for its foggy, austere appearance.

[8] *Lohrville Enterprise 3/7/35 (25 years-ago-today)*, "John Cavanaugh, a prosperous farmer of Union township, met with an accident Wednesday evening of last week which resulted in his death at 3 o'clock Saturday morning. He was returning home from Wightman with a load of tile and the spring seat becoming disarranged, he attempted to fix it without stopping the team. It is supposed he overbalanced and fell headlong to the ground, the heavy seat striking him on the forehead. When neighbors reached him, he was unconscious and bleeding profusely. He was taken to his home and medical aid was secured but his injuries were of such a nature that but little could be done for him. Mr. Cavanaugh was a man highly respected in the community and his neighbors will mourn his demise. The funeral occurred from the Catholic Church at Lohrville Monday morning."

[9] Bill Cavanaugh died at 93 on the same day his father had died 74-years earlier, February 21.

[10] The Butlers were bricklayers who began a construction company that built, among other things, the Minneapolis airport. They later invested in iron mills becoming very wealthy. During WWII, they built 17 ships out of Duluth that participated in the D-Day invasion. They eventually became very influential in Minnesota, democratic politics.

[11] In November and December of 1871, the Board of Police and Fire Commissioners investigated the cause of the Great Chicago Fire. Mrs. O'Leary testified on November 24, "I was in bed myself and my husband and five children when this fire commenced. I was the owner of them five cows that was burnt and the horse, wagon, and harness. I had two tons of coal and two tons of hay. I had everything that I wanted in for the winter. I could not save five cents worth of anything out of the barn, only that Mr. Sullivan got out a little calf. The calf was worth eleven dollars on Saturday morning. I

refused eleven dollars for the calf, and it was sold afterwards for eight dollars. I didn't save one five cents out of the fire. I could not tell anything of the fire, only that two men came by the door. I guess it was my husband got outside the door and he ran back to the bedroom and said, "Kate the barn is afire!" I ran out and the whole barn was on fire ... upon my word, I could not tell anymore about the fire."

[12] Clark Mollenhoff was born in Burnside, Iowa and his mother's family was from Lohrville and spent summers on his grandfather's farm next to the Cavanaughs. In 1957, he won the Pulitzer Prize as a Washington D. C. investigative reporter, "For his lengthy inquiry into labor union racketeering, thereby assisting congressional investigations." He worked for Cowles Publications and the *Des Moines Register and Tribune.* He served for a time in the White House during the Nixon administrations and later in life, "Mulley," was a favorite among his students at Washington and Lee University in Lexington, Virginia until his death on March 2, 1991 (Jim Gordon, my brother-in-law's brother, had "Mulley" as a teacher there). Clark Mollenhoff wrote many poems stemming from his experiences in Lohrville. Christa McAuliffe took a copy of his poem, *Teacher,* with her on her Challenger flight into space on January 28, 1986. He's buried in Lohrville. His grandfather, James Clark, owned the farm that Grandpa and Grandma purchased after Paul's death. Mollenhoff bought the acreage with the barn on it from Dad. Clark sided the barn in metal and began constructing his personal library in the hay mount. He only succeeded in building the steps to the hay mount before his death. He constructed a sign Pat helped Dad mount on the front of the barn identifying his grandfather, James Clark, and William Cavanaugh as "Pioneer Iowa Farmers." Mollenhoff's poem, *The Old Barn,* was about this barn.

[13] Merle Stephenson died in high school of an infected blister acquired from playing football. Though penicillin was already discovered, it wasn't in wide use at that time.

[14] Robert Cavanaugh joined the Royal Canadian Air Force on October 14, 1941 in Montreal. His father was shown as "deceased" and mother as, "Catherine Kiley." He trained in Toronto, Canada before being shipped overseas where he served as a gunner with the 405 Squadron based in Dedden, Essex, England. According to his military records I received from the Canadian government, he was killed in an accident 2½ miles south of Newport in his Halifax II bomber on November 17, 1942, weeks before Paul's death. Onboard were Sgt. A. J. Dolding (pilot), Landau (navigator), W. A. MacDonald (bomb-aimer), Sgt. H. G. Richards (WOP/AG), H. T.

Jackson (F/E) and Sgt. Robert Cavanaugh (A/G - R135149). MacDonald and Jackson were able to bail out of the aircraft. MacDonald was uninjured, Jackson injured, and the other men were killed. The aircraft was flying at 5000' with poor visibility due to low clouds that day. MacDonald reported, "mid-upper gunner Sgt. Cavanaugh, while 'fooling with the guns' fired a burst into the port inner engine. This engine immediately seized, caught fire, and all hydraulics operated at same moment, wheels, flaps, and bomb-doors opening. The aircraft then apparently went into a flat spin to port. No instruction was received from the Captain to abandon the aircraft." Additional notes were added to Robert's record, "A/G (Cavanaugh) apparently not impressed with importance of 'Fire Safe' Mechanism." From 10/14/42 we read, "Severely reprimanded for failing to obey order." A memorial service was held at the base on Saturday, November 21, 1942 before the internment at Saffron Walden cemetery three miles away. The men were buried next to one another. Robert had not undertaken a mission at the time of his death, but the 405th squadron took part in the historic 1,000-bomber raid on Cologne, Germany.

[15] Years later, Grandma was shot in her foot getting out of her car when the .22 Russ Bachman had in the backseat accidentally fired. Will Cavanaugh accidently shot himself in the foot by the same gun several years ago.

[16] In November of 2011, Ryan and I flew into Omaha en route to visit Mom, but first stopped at Bernice and Susan Chezlak's home. During our visit, Bernice confirmed what I had heard: Paul had a girlfriend of nearly two years. Bernice also knew her name, Delores (Dee) Wiederhold of Carroll. There were Wiederholt's in Lake View/Auburn but they were the "t" Weiderholts, not the "d" Weiderholds. I finally reached a Donald Wiederhold of Carroll who told me Dee was his aunt and was the woman we were looking for. She died eight years earlier (about 2003). Dee had married a plumber in Carroll named Roy Hammers. Roy and Dee had a large family but with Roy passing very early in their marriage, Dee became a single mother of nine kids. Their daughter, Barb Hammers, was in Chris Siemann's class (my age). Johnny was a good friend of Paul Siemann and lived with him "on and off" for years. Dee worked as a secretary at Saint Peter and Paul's. Paul Siemann remembers her being under a lot of stress and that she didn't talk much. Charlotte Heinrich recalls that during her student nursing days, she attended to a patient in the Carroll hospital who was suffering from a rash infection. The patient recognized Charlotte's maiden name and said she dated Paul Cavanaugh. It was Dee Hammers. Charlotte remembered one comment Dee made from her hospital bed regarding Paul, "He was a brick."

[17] We're not sure when they would have heard the news of the April 18th Dolittle attack on Tokyo which occurred the day before, perhaps shortly after boarding.

[18] I stumbled on the Grand Valley State University Veterans History Project and contacted them asking for New Guinea vets I could interview. Most of the living vets are in Michigan since they were with the Michigan National Guard unit. Earl Smestad, Wellington Homminga, Woodrow Tromp, Robert and Esther Van Hammen, and Shirley Weber were among the vets I had the privilege to interview.

[19] I met Paul Murphy on a trip to Indianapolis during the spring of 1988. He had been a survivor of the *USS Indianapolis*. The ship had secretly delivered the world's first operational atomic bomb to Tinian Island on July 26, 1945. From there it went to Guam and then was deployed to Leyte, Philippines to prepare for the invasion of Japan. Between Guam and Leyte, at 12:14 a.m. on July 30, 1945, the *USS Indianapolis* was torpedoed by a Japanese submarine in the Philippine Sea and sank in 12 minutes. Of 1,196 men on board, approximately 300 went down with the ship. The remainder, about 900 men, were left floating in shark-infested waters with no lifeboats and most with no food or water. Four days later, only 316 men were still alive. The ships Captain McVay was wrongly court-martialed for not zigging and zagging, the only commander during WWII to have been court-martialed but was later exonerated. Paul Murphy passed away in 2010.

[20] As late as World War II the line-crossing ceremony was still rough and sometimes included the "Devil's Tongue," an electrified piece of metal poked into the sides of Pollywogs. Beatings were common, usually with wet fire hoses. The *Lurline* Pollywogs outnumbered the Shellback seaman onboard so, according to one vet, a handful from each company was selected for the rite of passage. They all received certificates of having passed the equator and the initiation process, however.

[21] In May of 1942, the Japanese decided to capture Port Moresby. From Rabaul on New Britain, Japanese troop transports were dispatched. The American deciphered the Japanese naval code and hurried their forces to intercept them in what became known as the Battle of the Coral Sea. It was the first naval battle in history where neither side came within sight of the other but both sustained tremendous damages. Though a tie, the Americans were successful in turning the transports back to Rabaul.

[22] Indexes such as the lifestyle magazine *Monocle*, the Mercer Quality of Living Survey, and the Economist Intelligence Unit rank Melbourne as the #1 city in the world to live (or among the top ten) with Adelaide close behind.

[23] To show their appreciation for the Americans, the City of Adelaide threw a huge 4th of July parade. The soldiers remembered how throngs threw confetti out their windows and cheered for them as heroes.

[24] June 7th was an eventful day, Paul's 25th birthday and the day the Japanese invaded the Aleutian Islands.

[25] When Paul spoke of you and his brothers and sisters, I asked him if he would give me your address so that I might write you. I hope that I am not taking undue liberty in writing you, but I gathered during our conversation that Paul is of the opinion that you are not receiving news of him, and I felt I must write you right away. Paul left about half an hour ago to visit our neighbors. Paul will be off again to "Goodness knows where" in the near future, and we are hoping he will write us just to let us know how he is jogging along. He appears to be in perfect health and cheerful. We only regret not knowing him sooner and so enjoyed lots more of his company, however, he may come back sometime, and we hope to keep in touch with him ... We certainly had reason to fear the Japs move southward, but with the arrival of American troops and no end of equipment, now have a feeling of security. How we do earnestly pray for peace and the return of all these fine young men to their dear ones. So many of them are far too young to face the temptations, some so much weaker than others. You must be comforted in knowing that your son is the strong steady type, and we trust he will be spared through all to return home to you in perfect health. My mother, husband, and son join with me in sending you greetings and every good wish. I am yours very sincerely,

— (Mrs. E. Clayton; Prospect, South Australia)

[26] Rockhampton has a marker in town showing the latitudinal location of the Tropic of Capricorn. The Tropic of Capricorn is outside of the town but was moved into town to accommodate tourists. During the World War II, a U.S. army base was established outside the city; it hosted up to 70,000 servicemen en route to combat throughout the Pacific Ocean.

[27] Ward's Drome ("5 Mile Drome") was located five miles outside of Port Moresby. It was named after Australian Lt. Col. K. H. Ward who was involved in its construction and who was killed on the Kokoda trail. Its

wartime code name was "Maple" (U.S. Army APO 929). The airport was built in the middle of 1942 with Australian and U.S. Army engineers. The airport consisted of two parallel 6,000' x 100' runways. During 1943, Ward's Drome was the busiest airfield in the entire Southern Hemisphere, used mainly by cargo and larger aircraft.

[28] During World War II, American soldiers ascribed to various female broadcasters on Japanese radio the acumen, "Tokyo Rose." One woman became known as "the" Tokyo Rose. Iva Ikuko Toguri of Chicago was an American citizen who happened to be visiting a relative in Japan when the War broke out. The Japanese authorities tried to force her to renounce her American citizenship which she refused to do. She finally found work as a typist for Radio Tokyo where American and Australian prisoners of war were forced to broadcast radio propaganda. Toguri secured black-market food, supplies, and medicine for these POW's who, from time to time tried to sneak in pro-American messages into their programs whenever possible. When the radio station decided to go with a female voice, Toguri was chosen. After the war, she was viewed a traitor, tried, fined $10,000, and sent to prison for ten years. Upon her release, she fought for two years against being deported and after winning that effort moved back to Chicago to run the family business. She would ultimately be given a full pardon from President Gerald Ford in 1977.

[29] The circle just above the double arrows (the American front), shows the Japanese position. Arrows show American advances. The circle just above the Japanese position marks the location of the Huggin's Roadblock. The picture shows a single arrow marking the American flanking movement to the right. Not shown would be Paul's flanking movement to the left. Company I & K's left flanking motion ultimately secured the Roadblock. The diagram shows a circle above the Roadblock which represents Japanese reinforcements from Buna and Sanananda meant to break the Roadblock. Another American Roadblock was established behind that Japanese advance and represented by yet another circle. Girua River parallels the Sanananda Trail to the right.

[30] Mollenhoff approached Dad to purchase Grandpa's homesite. The barn was all that was left. Mollenhoff had plans to build his personal library in the barn. He sided the barn with red metal, he built a stairway into the hay mount, and then passed away. The property was willed to the Iowa Historical Society who did not want to keep it up. Dad purchased the property back from the Iowa Historical Society at a profit. Mollenhoff designed a sign on

the barn that identified his grandfather, James Clark, and Grandpa Cavanaugh, as early pioneer farmers.

Made in the USA
San Bernardino, CA
14 February 2019